WADSWORTH PHILOSOF

ON

PLATO

John E. Peterman
William Paterson University

Wadsworth
Thomson Learning

Australia • Canada • Mexico • Singapore • Spain
United Kingdom • United States

This book is gratefully dedicated to my parents
Alice E. Peterman and Robert W. Peterman.

Printed in the United States of America
  2 3 4 5 6 7 03 02 01 00

For permission to use material from this text, contact us:
Web: http://www.thomsonrights.com
Fax: 1-800-730-2215
Phone: 1-800-730-2214

For more information, contact:
Wadsworth/Thomson Learning, Inc.
10 Davis Drive
Belmont, CA 94002-3098
USA
http://www.wadsworth.com

ISBN: 0-534-57608-7

Table of Contents

Preface   i

Introduction   1

Chapter One: Plato's Life and Times   11

    Life in 5th and 4th century Athens   16

        The Polis   16

        War   17

        Greek Education   19

        Rhetoric – Part I   24

        Religion   28

Chapter Two: Philosophy   32

    I. Death   34

    II. Life   45

    III. Rhetoric – Part II   57

Chapter Three: The Medium of the Dialogue   69

    I. Literary Background   70

    II. Frames and Settings   73

    III. Conversation   76

    IV. Stories and Myths   82

    V. Socratic Irony   85

Selected Bibliography   92

Preface

In a business where truth is rarely accepted without a fight, philosophy does have this one truth, that most often philosophers really do need to use all those words in their writing and that we need to read them all if we are ever going to learn what they are trying to tell us. This book is not intended as a substitute for the reading of Plato. If anyone tries to use it this way, they will get what they deserve; they will be confused, liable to public ridicule and robbed of the opportunity to trade ideas with one of the world's most interesting thinkers, writers and conversationalists. This book will relate some of the ways in which I have come to speak with Plato. If readers want to know what Plato really meant, they will have to ask him for themselves.

A preface is usually a short account of what readers should be aware of before they begin reading a book, yet Socrates is two-thirds of the way through the *Republic* when he announces that all the work they have done is only the prelude to their real inquiry. Some topics require more of an orientation than others. As the reading of Plato is one of the most extraordinary of philosophical experiences, this preface may be longer than expected.

An introductory text on Plato's thought must begin with the problem of how his writings are to be read. We are not sure what to make of a philosopher who writes dramatized conversations. In philosophy we are not used to either drama or conversation in our readings and are subsequently somewhat leery of both. How did Plato select the cast for each of his dialogues? How does their presence influence the topics under discussion? Which of the characters speaks for Plato--or for anyone else? What is the relation between the actions and our understanding of the ideas presented? How are the dialogues connected, if at all? How is this writing to be read?

What little we know from Plato himself about his life and his intentions for his writing comes from comments in several letters attributed to him, at least some of which are forgeries. Some near contemporaries, especially Aristotle, have also commented on Plato's thought, but without further confirmation, we cannot evaluate the neutrality or polemics of these comments and thus their accuracy. Neither Plato nor anyone else seems to be able to give us any certain guidance on how his writings should be read.

Most of us also have few clear ideas about what life was like and how topics were discussed in Athens when Plato wrote 2500 years ago. Did everyone believe that gods directed human affairs from atop Mount Olympus? Did these people who had so much time available for conversations ever do any work? The dialogues discuss issues which seem quaint and out of date or at least out of style, such as the immortality of the soul, the acquisition of virtue, and the importance of citizenship. And they use fantastic myths to explain things just when we want an argument. Did Plato's audience (did Plato himself?) really believe these tall tales about life in the afterlife of Hades?

The strategies suggested for moving from these initial questions to some basis for approaching his works quickly begin to multiply and to confuse. Some determine the significant events in Plato's biography and then show how these directed the development and expression of his ideas, as Plato's experiences in Sicily as a political consultant shaped his political theory. Some extract the key issue or idea, either as revealed in autobiography or agreed to by scholarly consensus, and use this to orient the discussion, as many navigate Plato's writings using the Theory of Forms for their compass. Some, while engaging in the current debates in philosophy, assign previous thinkers a role (often full of straw, that is, easy to pull apart) in these, such as that Plato was a rationalist, idealist, dualist, etc.

The dream that we can open a book and in some way directly encounter the writer has a powerful attraction for us. Plato initially encourages this fantasy. Each dialogue takes us right into the middle of some action. A trial or religious festival is going on, an execution is about to occur, a walk either inside or outside of the city leads to a conversation. We are caught up in an activity that seems almost too direct, and, as we try to orient ourselves, more questions arise. Why has the author selected this event for us to witness? What already happened or will happen next? Who are these people? How are they related? What do they want with each other? What is at stake here?

Novels have taught us to read through an omniscient narrator who will entertain us with her story. We accept the authority of the author without thinking. A Platonic dialogue seems initially similar to this, but as narrator Plato always remains well hidden and as entertainment the plots of the stories are often unsatisfying. Socrates, for example, is able to convince everyone he meets, yet cannot convince the jury at the trial for his own life. An inquiry into how we can develop human virtue ends up making it the gods' responsibility. A long-winded and not very successful attempt to prove the immortality of the soul concludes with the death of the main participant. An apparently self-serving elevation of philosophers to political leadership ends with a discussion about art. There is something unsettling in these stories. The writer has pulled us in only to eventually push us back. All is not revealed, transparent and available. Diotima's divine instructions, when Socrates passes them on to Alcibiades, do not change his life. Socrates' followers who hear his final defense of the soul's immortality still reject it and weep at his death. Plato's "theory of Forms", supposedly the foundation of his work, is criticized by the most famous philosopher of his generation.

We want our story lines to be straightforward. If there are to be any puzzles, we want them clearly identified and readily solvable, such as the hour-long mystery on television or the pulp fiction thriller. We expect our reading to be as direct and literal as any other event in our daily lives. The day is sunny, so it should be warm outside. The words spoken by weathermen, teachers or lovers should be believable at their face value. A typical behavior should have its typical meaning, such as Alcibiades' drunken entrance at Agathon's symposium or Phaedrus taking his exercise around the city's walls.

But the sun's light does not always make the day hot. The lover's promise too often is false, and the observed behavior may be only an act. The world is not self-revealing in any simple and immediate fashion. Our judgment is required to interpret the meaning of the words and deeds around us. One aspect of philosophy is the development of this judgment. To this end, the reading of Plato's works is a series of exercises; they develop our judgment as they force us to apply it in their interpretation.

This book is intended as a guide to help understand and engage in these exercises. It is meant to be useful rather than comprehensive. My principle of inclusion is whatever material helps one to be able to read Plato's work. This is not the same as providing interpretations of what Plato must have meant. This book will succeed if it provides the tools and direction for its readers to begin developing their own interpretations of Plato's writings and the criticisms of his many commentators, including, of course, the comments in this book.

I should say something about the organizing principles of this work. The first principle is to provide a variety of examples from a variety of dialogues, even though many readers may have read only one or two. Although each dialogue can be understood on its own terms, connections with other dialogues are often provocative and give directions for further inquiry. The intended audience for the book is readers who have some acquaintance, however slight, with Plato and desire to further this relationship. If there are passages that sound narrow or technical, I have tried to make these supplemental to the main lines of the book.

Some familiar aspects of what many people have said about Plato may not appear at all in this book or not as early as the reader might expect. Thus a second principle is that the material is presented in a sequence moving from simple to more complex. Many of the most difficult ideas about Plato are discussed at the beginning of books or courses, often with little preparation, and result in audiences feeling that Plato was more dogmatic than he need be. For instance, complex ideas such as reincarnation and recollection seem to demand some prior proof for the immortality of the soul, yet although several such proofs are discussed, none prove acceptable. We are left in a position of feeling pity for this inept and deluded Plato who had some interesting ideas but often seems to be asking us to believe more than he can prove.

This leads to a third principle that the ancient Athenians were more like us than different from us, especially in their reasoning. Reading Aristophanes, Euripides and Thucydides in addition to Plato will help readers appreciate the sophistication and complexity of Greek thought and expression.

It is common today, though not necessary, to believe that Plato changed and improved some of his most fundamental ideas during his long life, so that scholars gravitate to the most developed versions as most distinctive of Plato's thought. This belief presents several problems. It tends to privilege his supposedly later writings, when the order and dates of his works have not been determined with certainty. It tends to divide the dialogues philosophically between early equals Socrates and later equals Plato, dissuading readers from finding a unified and coherent presentation across all of the dialogues. Finally, in its search for evolving ideas, it tends to look only at arguments in the dialogues and exclude other elements of the drama as not philosophical. Thus a fourth principle is that I will not assume either a particular chronological order of composition for the dialogues or that Plato's ideas, and our interpretation, must necessarily follow any pattern of development based upon such a chronology.

The fifth principle relates to the "arguments vs. drama" controversy just mentioned. I will approach the dialogues as each written in its entirety by a philosopher, that is, a person who for philosophical reasons wrote what he did and wrote in the way that he did. Thus in order to understand Plato's philosophy, one has to read all of what he wrote and examine why he wrote in this way. Our current forms of analysis tend to isolate the individual argument, just as we isolate the individual thinker. In Plato's dialogues we see thinking as a communal activity. This is reflected in the entire community of elements in the dialogue affecting what occurs in it.

A final principle is to discuss some of the current controversies in the interpretation of the dialogues, avoiding polemics if possible, to help readers be aware that they do not have to be held hostage by opinions expressed by scholarly experts. Often the explanations we hear are so clever that we forget that these are only opinions being presented and not facts. The danger from accepting the experts too soon is that the reader's own responses to the text are undermined and dismissed. The dialogues' dramatic presentation of ideas evokes more emotions than an essay, suggesting that these responses may be important for the reader's entrance into the text, just as they are for the character's entrance into the discussion.

The preface to all of my efforts in life has been my parents, Alice and Robert. They have been patient, generous and supportive. This book is dedicated to them. My wife Ellen is my best companion and editor; her wise advice is to leave most of the jokes on the cutting room floor. My son Jeremy explained the subtleties of Word. Many people read parts of the manuscript, and the suggestions of my colleagues

Angelo Juffras, Robert Talisse and Robert Tempio were most helpful. I hope this book is as much fun to read as it was to write.

Introduction

The safest general characterization of the European
philosophical tradition is that it consists of a series of
footnotes to Plato. I do not mean the systematic scheme of
thought which scholars have doubtfully extracted from his
writings. I allude to the wealth of general ideas scattered
through them. His personal endowments, his wide
opportunities for experience at a great period of civilization,
his inheritance of an intellectual tradition not yet stiffened
by excessive systematization, have made his writing an
inexhaustible mine of suggestion.
                                        - Whitehead[1]

How does one begin to discuss reading a philosopher like Plato
who has been read extensively and discussed intensively for 2500
years? To begin with a question seems to set the right environment, for
to discuss the reading of Plato is to embark on a rather wild ride where
the questions begin early and never seem to stop. That the work of
philosophy is similarly involved with finding complicated questions
and exploring where they may lead might not be mere coincidence.
Plato seems to try by any means possible to engage his readers in
philosophical activity. If debates about how he should be read furthers
this personal reflection and greater conscious contact with our beliefs,
then our present confusion of interpretations is all to the good. In fact,

he may have written in such a way that he planned for this confusion to be his legacy, his philosophical gift to his audience.

The questions begin early. Plato's philosophical writings are always conversations, either between characters who share their opinions in the story or between a narrator and an audience. Pick any of these dialogues, and the problem of Plato's presence or absence soon arises. Plato is writing all of these stories or accounts, but he carefully avoids appearing in them. He appears briefly in the audience at Socrates' trial, and in name appears in order to account for his absence on Socrates' death day. One does not expect a playwright or novelist, a Shakespeare or Tolstoi, to speak directly in his own voice during a story. Such intrusion by the author is often more annoying than helpful. A philosopher, however, is supposed to directly present his opinions and the arguments for believing them.

Now the questions multiply further. Why is Plato not present in his own voice? Is he hiding so as not to assume responsibility, so as to avoid the same fate as Socrates? Is he saying something about the nature of philosophy by refusing to take center stage? Or about the nature of education and our learning?

Maybe Plato just appears to be absent. He does not want his name involved, but he could appear in the guise of another character. Maybe he has a mouthpiece, a spokesman who voices his opinions in the story. Maybe he would give this character all of the best lines and make him his representative in his relations with the world. Most of the time the character "Socrates" seems to get the best lines and do the heavy thinking, but does this make him Plato's image of himself? And what are we to make of those dialogues where Socrates either does not have a main role or is absent? Certainly most writers do not have the same characters in all of their works, but if a character is usually present, then her absence or silence in a work requires an explanation. Also must a character be consistent in opinions and expressions in each appearance or might she say different things as her mood, audience or purpose changes? Would a character's ideas develop over time by dropping old ones and adopting new ones, or would they remain essentially the same while becoming more complex both in their expression and in relation to other ideas?

Plato does not provide us with the information to answer such questions, and so our imaginations begin to get ideas. We wish to speak with Plato and therefore need some explanation for where he might be found: who speaks for Plato, how much do they speak for Plato and why is the spokesperson not always the same character. Before we even get into what the characters are arguing about, we are engaging in the philosophical business of making judgments just by trying to figure out how to read these stories. We are beginning to bring our opinions to consciousness, formulate them clearly enough to examine them with another person and evaluate the resulting critique.

But is this really a serious problem how Plato happens to present his ideas? What do we care whose name is attached to an idea, so long as the idea is shown to be true or false. In *The Divine Comedy* when Dante has lost his sense of meaning and direction in life, it is his role model Virgil whose words move him to action, and it is his lover Beatrice's agreement to the journey which gives Dante the confidence to begin his trip through Hell. Who is making the argument is often all important in determining if the words are even heard, much less followed. The Virgil who successfully leads Dante through Hell is only an intermediary. He does not have all the answers and by his presence even creates some new questions, such as why virtuous pagans like Virgil must remain forever separated from God in Limbo. The virtuous Beatrice in Paradise will later give more answers, but it is Virgil who shakes Dante up and gets him started. When we meet Socrates in Plato's writings, is he the Virgil-like intermediary who stirs up his audience and gets them (and us) moving or does he inhabit the Paradise of the Forms and give us all the answers like Beatrice?

II.

Students' papers often begin "Plato, the greatest philosopher who ever lived" or "Plato, the famous Greek thinker." This provides them with some cover. They have an assignment to write about Plato, and they want to say something certain and, therefore, safe. Scholars who comment on Plato's works share this interest in being sure and safe. Since most scholars discuss other philosophers only in passing on their way to clarify their own ideas, they do not wish to take any distracting or embarrassing risks. Plato has long served as a point of orientation in philosophy, with "Platonist" serving as a common term of reference, suggesting approval or criticism depending on the current fashion in ideas. "Platonism" provides a safe, because generally accepted, account of Plato's writings. As with other understandings adjusted to the most readily accepted common denominator, the origin and contents of this one should be carefully examined before using it.

The development of this common and safe understanding of Plato has five main aspects: literal approach to the text, Plato speaks directly through a mouthpiece, Plato had a key idea central to all of his work (the Theory of Forms), Plato's ideas developed during his life which explains the inconsistencies in the literal understanding of his writings, and finally ancient commentators understood and accurately reported upon his work, especially Aristotle. Each of these aspects is controversial, and I will briefly describe some of the issues in these controversies that will be further developed in later chapters. The possibility of a literal approach is basic for the others and will receive the most attention.

I should note here that the intention of this book is to develop an environment where a plurality of readings of Plato is encouraged, since no current interpretation has proven to be the unique solution to all Platonic puzzles. I certainly have my preferences concerning which approaches are the most fertile, but also readily acknowledge that I have learned much from almost every careful discussion of these writings, regardless of which technical approach it follows. Plato is such a complex writer with so many dimensions to his work that our attention is overwhelmed when we begin to take them seriously. We need others to help us see all that there actually is.

A literal approach to a text reflects our habitual method for making our way through the world around us; we take it as it presents itself to us. Things and events in the world do not have extra meanings, such as symbolizing something else, unless we happen to be feeling poetic or profound and give such meanings to them. In reading we have a similar literal understanding of the words unless instructed otherwise. Libraries and bookstores appropriately distinguish fiction from non-fiction, guiding our expectations. Plato's dialogues are found with the rest of philosophy in the non-fiction area. Our expectation is that he will be as straightforward as an author of history or geography.

Although he presents historical figures participating in what are, at least sometimes, historical events (Socrates' trial, the religious festival of Bendis or Agathon's victory celebration), Plato makes sure we realize that he is telling stories about these people and that the amount of historical truth in them is uncertain. Only one dialogue mentions Plato as present. All the rest of his stories must be at least second hand and possibly fictitious. The *Symposium* begins with a framing conversation that brings to our attention how stories become altered in the retelling and the impossibility of any direct access to the facts for those of us who were not present. The account of these conversations and activities that we read is always Plato's version. Thus the first layer of literalness, that these events actually took place, is at least put into doubt.

4

The *Apology* is the dialogue most often taken as simple historical reporting. There is intriguing evidence on both sides of this issue, but neither can claim proof. The arguments in favor say that the recounting of Socrates' defense speech would have to be factual because Plato was a loyal student who would not correct his master (wishful thinking by the academic commentators) or that those present at the trial would later challenge any changes Plato tried to make (assuming the public expected this to be an accurate account, which is just what is to be proven). The arguments against say that the style matches other works by Plato and question why only this work would seek historical accuracy, while the others make use of historical fiction.

It is worth noting the basis of this debate, as it recurs endlessly in Platonic scholarship. We know little or nothing about Plato's intellectual development. Did he maintain a core set of beliefs throughout his life or did his beliefs evolve as he matured. Most of our own histories tend toward one or the other of these models, either an ever more complex response to similar problems or a series of new questions when old ones lose interest. That we know which type Plato must have been is wishful thinking by the disputing sides. We must examine carefully any interpretation based upon either constancy or change. They may reflect more about the interpreter than about Plato.

The first layer of literalness, historical accuracy, has been compromised. We are reading stories with complex relations to any actual time and place. But within the stories there is still a second layer of literalness giving us direct access, namely, that what people say is what they really believe. Lying and deception seem to be facts of our human condition, which is perhaps why Kant tried so desperately to neutralize their power. There is no way to tell in ordinary conversation when another person is telling the truth. From the beginning of the *Apology* where Socrates warns his audience that their judgment is already clouded by prejudice and stereotyping, to the repeated discussions of rhetoric and sophistry where plausibility challenges truth, to the semi-conscious lying of lovers in the *Symposium,* to the self-conscious lying for a good cause with the "noble lie" in the *Republic*, Plato continually reminds us that deception is a potential, if not actual, component of all conversation. Lying is an ever-present problem for Plato, as it is for all philosophy. We cannot just assume others are telling the truth or that their words give us access to their beliefs.

That the story is true or that the characters' words are true have both become problems rather than assurances. A third layer of literalness is that the author must have some direct way to speak his truth to us. If his own voice is not present, then the next most direct way is that he speaks through some representative. We believe that if philosophers are going to seek the truth, then they must always speak the truth. Plato, as a philosopher, must have a direct representative to convey his truth. Since Socrates is another philosopher (truth seeker/teller) and also has the most interesting lines, he must be Plato's mouthpiece. There are three problems with this. First if Socrates does speak for Plato, we are repeatedly warned that he does not always tell the truth. He claims In the *Symposium* that Diotima was his teacher, yet Aristophanes presents evidence that Socrates made up the story on the spot. In the *Phaedo* he claims to have proofs for the immortality of the soul, yet they all fall apart. And philosophers, like other lovers, claim that they have a right to lie in the appropriate circumstances, as in the "noble lie" of the *Republic*, so we must always be concerned if the present circumstance is one of those appropriate ones. The second problem merely extends this situation to Plato himself. If there is no need for Socrates to tell us the truth, there is equally none for Plato, so speaking through Socrates would make his words no more trustworthy.

And we must now face the third problem, like the third and most serious wave in the *Republic (472a)*, whether Plato actually does speak through Socrates? There must be some relation between the author and his most frequent and talkative character. How plausible is it that this relation is simply one of substitution, that Socrates represents Plato? Out of the dozens of arguments on this issue, I will briefly mention four. All arguments that Plato acted out of humility or respect in honoring his teacher with pride of place are wishful academic dreams. Good students can just as easily criticize their teachers, as many of these same commentators believe was the case with Aristotle toward Plato. Another belief, which students respond to, is that Plato wanted to philosophize without jeopardizing his life as Socrates had. If he speaks through another, then he cannot be held accountable. But if philosophy was such a politically dangerous pursuit in 4th century Athens, then to write any books promoting it, in one's own voice or another's, would be equally dangerous. Another version of using Socrates as a smoke screen is that Plato wanted his ideas to be seen as emanating from the great wise man Socrates. Since his audience was mostly younger people, they would not know what Socrates had actually said. Plato could initially pass off his own ideas as Socrates' and then, when they are accepted, reveal them as his own.

A more serious version of this approach leads to the fourth argument. The dialogues frequently address issues of authority in pedagogy. Does the teacher transfer her knowledge to the student or only offer guidance while the student has to somehow find the knowledge for himself? Meno in his dialogue repeatedly wants to be told the answers by Socrates who Meno is sure must know them. This echoes modern students' complaints about their senseless participation in "Socratic" discussions when the teacher knows the answers the whole time. Why does the teacher not handle the bundle of knowledge over to the student for insertion into his brain? The *Phaedo* highlights this issue with its Pythagorean background where the teacher is "Master" and learning by rote is played off against the Socratic probing of arguments in order to see where they lead. The situation in this dialogue is desperate; these students want to get the answers before this knowledge disappears along with the brain of their soon-to-be-executed teacher. Socrates responds with half a dozen provocative but ultimately unsuccessful arguments for the immortality of the soul. What sort of knowledge is Socrates teaching in these faulty arguments? Who is the teacher here: Plato, Socrates, his followers, the reader?

This last use of a mouthpiece complicates rather than clarifies Plato's ideas and purposes and thus does not serve the cause of literalness. It also introduces the further problem of irony. How do we know when Socrates is being serious? Philosophers are supposed to be serious, but Socrates at times is clearly putting on his interlocutor. Meno is from the boondocks of Greece, and when Socrates praises the worldly knowledge of their horse farmers, it is at least a challenge if not a joke. In the *Symposium* Socrates boasts that he is an expert in love matters, yet the woman he claims to be his teacher most likely never existed. As with lying, once irony becomes an option, it is virtually impossible to identify when it is or is not occurring in a conversation. What good is a mouthpiece who seems to intentionally and unpredictably play with telling the truth?

This more pervasive sense of creeping loss of clarity brings us to the fourth and final layer of literalness, that a text has some straightforward meaning expressed in a straightforward way. People write books for a reason and express this to their readers. Plato must have an agenda and tell us what it is. Commentators do offer simple explanations for each of the dialogues telling why Plato wrote this particular story. The *Apology* shows the nobility of Socrates' character. The *Meno* reveals Plato's application of his religious belief in reincarnation to the problem of knowledge with the resulting discovery of recollection. The *Republic* either defends his attempts to influence the politics of Syracuse, presents his political program as opposed to that of other Athenians such as Isocrates, or explains the superiority of philosophic intuition, especially in the image of the Cave. The *Phaedo* proves the immortality of the soul or offers another defense of Socrates or justifies philosophy as the best human occupation. The problem with the variety of these accounts is that if Plato's meaning were clear, then there should be more agreement as to the content of this unified explanation which leaves no part of the story unaccounted for. Why does Socrates emphasize the role of the Eleusinian Mysteries in the *Meno* and the *Symposium* when this religious belief rejects the reincarnation needed for Plato's discovery of recollection? Why does Socrates' own ideal city have no need for rulers, and only the later "fevered city" gives rise to the philosopher-kings? Why do Socrates and Protagoras in his dialogue reverse their beliefs? Such questions nag at our interpretations and refuse our attempts at simple organizational schemes.

There is a puzzle-like quality in Plato's writing. He seems to complicate his presentation, beginning with the choice of writing in dialogue, continuing through his mixture of good arguments in bad causes (the learning paradox) and bad arguments in good causes (immortality in the *Phaedo*) and finally his mythic turns, the telling of magical (the Ring of Gyges) or supernatural (Myth of Er in the afterlife) tales offered as some sort of philosophical contribution. The simple textbook explanations help get us started with a dialogue, but we must remain sensitive when our warning bells go off as more pieces of the story or argument fail to make sense. We will have to discuss further why Plato would not want his writings to have transparent meanings when we examine his understanding of philosophy. What does seem clear at this point is that the expectations of this fourth and final layer of literalness have been thwarted along with the others.

III.

Now that the ease and security of the literal approach has been denied to us, we need to find a second best approach, as Socrates describes in the *Phaedo*, when he had to find a second type of approach (a "second sailing") after the ease and security of explaining causal relations by simply perceiving them failed. (99d) He developed what he described as a hypothetical approach. He intuited a reasonable explanation for the events and then carefully reasoned from this explanation to all the details of the event in order to ascertain that none of the supposed facts of the case were inconsistent with the proposed explanation. If inconsistency did arise, both the assumed facts and the hypothesis would be re-examined to determine which needed to be corrected. Such an imposed explanation always remains subject to correction as our appreciation of the event and of the logical connections between our ideas evolves.

I propose a similar approach to the reading of Plato. That method which makes sense of the greatest part of the text while leaving the least of the text unexplained is best, while the amount and significance of those things left unexplained act as a limiting factor on our certainty. No individual dialogue should require another for its basic understanding, although similar dramatic events or arguments are worth comparing to see why they are repeated or changed. I have not yet found a reading, including my own, which makes sense of every element in any of the dialogues. Inevitably when teaching a dialogue, one of my students will ask an innocent question about some detail of the story which I had never noticed or had dismissed as not important. When one is reading a careful writer, and Plato does seem to take care with his characters, plots, and arguments, then it is important to keep track of details, especially the ones that seem odd.

One of the standard moves by a commentator is to say that some detail or section of a dialogue does not require any attention because it has no philosophical importance or interest, which only means it has no such interest to the person making this judgement. A second similar move is that any awkward details that do not fit the interpretation are dismissed as the author's lapses in care. If Plato does not agree with us or himself, it is said this is because his mind here wandered or failed him. These moves show the power of our theories in determining what we are even able to notice, much less consider. Plato's writings repeatedly address this problem of the reader's presuppositions, beginning with the opening of the *Apology* when Socrates challenges the jury to examine their prejudice that he is a clever rhetorician who twists words. He fears that his arguments will not even be heard due to his audience's considering them to be lies and thus of no interest.

Amateur scientists frequently make discoveries in their fields because they are able to be struck by what their more scholarly mature colleagues know to ignore. Students should be warned that the explanations of experts tend to destroy many of the ideas and undermine many of the observations that first time readers find in a text. Books like this one which purport to explain Plato's ideas or introductions to an edition of a Platonic dialogue should only be read after the reader has had time to develop her own questions after reading Plato's own words. To remove all traces of the puzzle in Plato's writing is to miss one of the essential elements in its reading.

In the *Theaetetus* Socrates suggests that in "wondering: this is where philosophy begins and nowhere else" (155d). Meno in his dia-

9

logue only begins to act as a participant rather than a predator in their conversation after he finds a question that causes him to wonder instead of to calculate his advantage (96d and 97d). The storytellers in the *Phaedo* and the *Symposium* seem to be in awe of their topic and to be reciting much more than they can explain. Plato does not present philosophy as user friendly and simple; he shows it as at times an overwhelming experience and a struggle.

Textual Concerns

In the margins of most modern editions of Plato there are numbers and letters which are the standard system for referring to passages from Plato's writings. These are called "Stephanus numbers" after the edition of 1578 by Henri Estienne (Stephanus in Latin) where they first appeared. In this book these numbers are used in parentheses following a quotation or reference in order to identify it.

Most of the quoted material comes from the wonderful recent edition *Plato Complete Works* edited by John Cooper and published by Hackett. For a reasonable price readers can have a one-volume collection of all of Plato's works, including those dozen or so now commonly thought to be forgeries. In some cases I have chosen to use translations not included in Cooper. The following list gives these editions.

Gorgias, trans. W. Helmhold, Indianapolis: Bobbs-Merrill, 1952.
Phaedrus, trans. W. Hamilton, New York: Penguin, 1973.
Protagoras, ed. G. Vlastos, Indianapolis: Bobbs-Merrill, 1956.
Republic, trans. A. Bloom, New York: Basic, 1968.
Symposium, trans. W. Hamilton, New York: Penguin, 1951.

Notes

1. A.N.Whitehead, *Process and Reality: An Essay in Cosmology* (New York: Free Press, 1978) 39.

1

Plato's Life and Times

Plato is for us moderns the consummate expression of Greece.
But what is Greece? For us, it is a group of literary
monuments suspended in time, together with the archeological
remains discovered during the last century. The documents are
all we really know.
- J.H. Randall [1]

The facts that we know about Plato's life are relatively few. That
he lived for 80 years (427-347 B.C.) seems innocent enough until we
realize that this was the standard length for a well-lived life used by
ancient biographers. This standard also included significant life events
at 20-year intervals. That Plato met Socrates at age 20, established his
school called the Academy or first traveled to Sicily at age 40 and
wrote what many consider his masterpiece, the *Republic,* at age 60
does seem very convenient but not implausible.

About his family we know that he was born into social and material comfort. His father Ariston, who died early in Plato's life, traced
his lineage back though Codrus, the last king of Athens, and ultimately
to the god Poseidon. His mother Perictione's genealogy included Solon,
the revered political reformer of the early 500's who established most
of the laws and institutions for the Athenian democratic state. His family had an illustrious political past and a still active though more am-

11

biguous political presence during Plato's later youth. Perictione's cousin Critias and brother Charmides were infamous as members of the Thirty Tyrants, the oligarchic (meaning rule by "the few", usually the rich) government (404-403 B. C.) imposed by Sparta to rule Athens following its defeat in the Peloponnesian War. Plato had two brothers Adeimantus and Glaucon, the main speakers in the *Republic*, a sister Potone who was the mother of Speusippus, Plato's successor as head of the Academy, and a half brother Antiphon who trained horses, one of Plato's common examples in his writings.

A. E. Taylor summarizes best what we know of Plato's early life and adulthood. "The actual history of Plato's life up to his sixtieth year is almost a blank".[2] Ancient biographers tell us that he traveled to Egypt and Italy, that he studied mathematics and religion, and that he came under the influence of the ideas of Parmenides or Heraclitus or Pythagoras. All of this is interesting but not certain. From his social position we can infer some activities, such as he would have participated in the Athenian Army, probably the cavalry due to his social and economic position, during the last few years of the Peloponnesian War. In the *Seventh Letter*, possibly by Plato, it says that he was invited to participate in the rule of the Thirty Tyrants but disgusted by their aims and methods. He was again interested in politics when democracy was restored but soon soured when its leaders were involved in the trial and execution of Socrates.

A career in the army, like his brothers, or in politics, like his uncle, was certainly open to him. But he rejects these public lives. As Socrates says in the *Apology*, "A man who really fights for justice must lead a private, not a public, life if he is to survive for even a short time" (32a). In the *Republic* Socrates repeats his warning that "no one who minds the business of the cities does anything healthy" (496c) and offers this image of the philosopher's place on the edge of the world.

> Taking all this (political injustice) into the calculation, he
> keeps quiet and minds his own business--as a man in a storm,
> when dust and rain are blown about by the wind, stands aside
> under a little wall. (496d)

What is it that turned Plato from his public career to his retreat to philosophy? On the same page in the *Republic* Socrates goes on to discuss how people come to join the small group that pursues philosophy. If people excel in both mind and body, it is almost impossible for them not to apply their talents to the socially prominent and rewarding paths to success. The bewitching spell of social and political power must be broken before the less immediate charms of philosophy can be experienced. This theme is frequently repeated in such characters as Meno, Alcibiades, and Charmides, none of whom were able to finally escape this spell. Socrates says the spell can in rare cases be broken but only by exile, by growing up apart from the ambitions of politics, by becoming physically disabled, by realizing the limits of whatever art one is practicing (remember in the *Apology* that an expert in any area tends to think that she is an expert in other areas as well) or in Socrates' even more unusual situation, by his prohibiting *daimon* or guardian spirit which warned him away from a public career. The political execution of his friend and mentor Socrates could certainly have disillusioned Plato with politics. In the *Seventh Letter,* genuine or not, Plato offers this plausible reason for his break from political life.

But just because something makes sense does not mean that it actually happened. This is the motto that we must keep before us with respect to all Plato biography and attempts to link the events of his life to the themes and developments in his writing. Most commentators want Plato's life to have a plot; most of us would like our lives to have a plot, a thread of meaning that provides guidance and security. But reconstructions of Plato's life are often based upon a reader's selection of favorite (but not historically proven) anecdotes, filled in with probabilities and supported with such circular reasoning as this argument defending the *Second Letter* as genuine. "A strong argument for the genuineness of the letter is the fact that it throws a great deal of light on a particular stage in the relation of Plato and Dionysius that is not illuminated by the other letters." [3]In other words, the author wants this information to be historical because its content is useful for his purposes.

Amid the succession of young men whom we find conversing with Socrates in the dialogues, including some who seem to be stretching their youth beyond its limits such as Agathon and Phaedrus, we gain a picture of what it was like to grow up in Athens during the Peloponnesian War. Our search for glimpses of Plato among these youth is complicated by the details of their actual historical natures and by the fact that Plato seems to be identify himself in opposition to these others as one of those who actually turned around (converted) and followed philosophy. Alcibiades in the *Symposium* is the portrait that I feel comes closest to autobiography. His reflections on how Socrates impressed himself on others and how they tried to interact with him have an intensely personal ring to them. It is essential in the reading of Plato to be sensitive to and keep record of such personal responses as this. They are the rudimentary connections which direct further inquiry and when successful lead us deeper into the meaning of the text. But they are not arguments. Whether we get a glimpse of Plato here is only an interesting conjecture. What is clear is that Plato repeatedly shows us his contemporaries who were exposed to philosophy but rejected it, while he, for whatever reason, embraced it.

The internal time frame of the dialogues, the dates when their action is supposed to have occurred, is always before the death of Socrates. This seems not so surprising since Socrates is a character in most of these writings. But this is also the period during which Plato was attracted to but not committed to philosophy. Each of the dialogues has as one of its dimensions this question of the nature and value of the philosophic life. The one experience of Plato's youth that he repeatedly shares with us is this confrontation with philosophy. The other details of his life, and by implication of ours, seem to be the arbitrary portions which the gods do or do not bestow on us.

The quotation above from Prof. Taylor suggests a distinction between what we know of Plato's life before and after he turned 60. The two events that happened in this year were that Plato's *Letters*, if genuine, give an account of his trips to Syracuse during this time and second, that Aristotle became a pupil in Plato's Academy and thus our primary source of first hand information about Plato. The *Letters* describe three visits by Plato to Syracuse. The first occurred when Plato was 40. He met Dion, a young relative of the ruler Dionysius I, who was dissatisfied with the luxurious lifestyle around him and eagerly listened to Plato's ideas on intellectual satisfaction and self-control. They parted friends, and on the ascension of Dionysius II, Dion asked Socrates to return and educate the new ruler as he had done twenty years before with Dion himself. The hope that a more rational (and thus self-controlled) ruler would help to create a more rational (and thus stable) government induced Plato to undertake this task, although his pupil had already been corrupted by 30 years of indulgent living. Dionysius eagerly pursued his studies as a pastime, but they had no influence on his ruling. He continued his politics of personal gain and intrigue, first exiling Dion and then confiscating his lands and forcing his wife to remarry. Plato realized that he was being used by Dionysius and returned to Athens. Seven years later Plato tried once more to reconcile Dion and Dionysius, as well as philosophy and politics, and visited Syracuse one last time. His relations with Dionysius deteriorated further until he was practically kept under house arrest and grudgingly permitted to return home. Plato maintained his relationship with Dion, who several years later led a successful revolt in Syracuse, only to be assassinated in turn.

To argue from historical biography to philosophical biography is like the futile attempts to derive ought from is. That Plato went to Syracuse, almost all scholars would agree. That the events happened as the *Seventh Letter* states, many would agree with. That the conception, development and significance of the *Republic, Laws* or other dialogues can be understood because of these journeys is highly controversial. In the *Republic* Socrates introduces the famous idea of the philosopher-king midway through the dialogue.

> Unless the philosophers rule as kings or those now called
> kings and chiefs genuinely and adequately philosophize, and
> political power and philosophy coincide in the same place,...
> there is no rest from ills for the cities, nor I think for human
> kind, nor will the regime we have now described in speech
> ever come forth from nature, insofar as possible, and see the
> light of the sun. (473e)

The *Seventh Letter* certainly expresses the same idea.

> The classes of humans will have no cessation from evils until
> either the class of those who are right and true philosophers
> attains political supremacy, or else the class of those who hold
> power in the state becomes, by some dispensation of the gods,
> really philosophic. (326b)

But this letter does not clarify what Plato thought he was doing in Syracuse, whether he was implementing the blueprint for an ideal city, creating a philosophic ruler to bring eternal peace and justice, or just trying to bring more rational law and order to a decadent, capricious and weak city whose fall to the barbarians (those who do not speak Greek) would further weaken the security of the Greek presence in Italy. Or maybe his involvement was an act of friendship and more about Dion than Dionysius. Plato's presence in Sicily could signify his acting in the practical politics of his day or in the fantasy of his ideal imaginings, just as his composition of the *Republic* remains similarly ambiguous. Neither the visit nor the book seem to be able to explain the other, though many people have tried. Plato's biography provides a few clues but no real program for how we are to read his work.

Life in 5th and 4th century Athens

When full and direct information about what a person is writing and why is not available, we need to gather as much indirect information as bears upon these works. Plato's biography has provided only limited clues, such as his relation with Socrates that we will examine further in the next chapter. Since stories in the dialogues occur in actual historical contexts, more clues may be gathered by knowing something about the times and places where these occur. To study and understand the culture of ancient Athens, as with any culture, is the work of a lifetime. To become seriously involved with Plato is to become involved with the religious practices, political and social practices, literature, political history and intellectual history of 450-350 B. C. I will offer a short discussion of each of these areas to help orient our immediate reading and suggest that the reader further consult a good introduction on ancient Greek culture to develop a more complete picture. A very readable one is H. D. F. Kitto's *The Greeks*.

The Polis

Greece is a land with many natural geographical boundaries and defenses: islands, mountain valleys and coastal plains divided by rivers and steep, rocky hills. In each of these centers a small and stable population can support life with relative ease, if not luxury, in the temperate climate. Athens was by far the largest of these with 20,000 male citizens and a total population including families, resident aliens and slaves of 350,000 in 430, while many cities had less than 5000 citizens. These centers grew up independently from each other and became each its own political unit, a city-state or *polis*.

Each *polis* had its own patron gods (Poseidon for Sparta and Athena for Athens), own economy (agriculture in Sparta and commerce in Athens, which imported most of its food from the Black Sea) and own government (oligarchy in Sparta and its allies, democracy in Athens and its allies) which would include different constitutions, laws and punishments. The cities did regularly unite, complete with truces and safe passage guarantees, to celebrate certain national religious and athletic festivals as the Olympic games.

Since farms could not readily expand beyond the geographical boundaries, the opportunities for younger children to inherit land were limited, as was the food supply and the population growth. Early Greek

16

cities organized their excess and landless population into a group who were willing to move and establish an independent daughter city, related to the mother city by blood and politics but not usually economically. After the mainland, Asia Minor and the Aegean islands were occupied, the colonists ventured to Sicily and southern Italy following the coast up to France, founding such cities as Marseilles, Nice, Monaco, Naples and Syracuse. This area of the northern Mediterranean over which the Greeks settled came to be called Greater Greece.

Cities both new and old needed political organization for which there was not a standard model. The despots of Persia were a sort of negative model that some Greek tyrants tried to imitate when they gained power, but most cities were ruled under a written constitution. Prominent citizens, such as Dracon or Solon in Athens, were sometimes called upon to rewrite the city's laws when social unrest, particularly by the landless poor, threatened the political stability. When new cities were founded or old ones reconstituted, political thinkers from around the Greek world would be invited either singly or in a contest to suggest a new constitution. New sets of laws and government could also be imposed on a city defeated in war: democracies by Athens, oligarchies by Sparta and despotisms by Persia.

War

The settings and action in Plato's dialogues are suffused with an almost golden light; people seem to have nothing better to do than to sit or stand around and chat. Sometimes people are just coming from or going to wars (Socrates in the *Charmides* or Meno in his dialogue) or appointments (Euthyphro or Socrates in the *Meno*) or home or death. But these activities rarely intrude into the dialogue itself, with few exceptions, as when Socrates is put to death. The dialogues seem to take place during some privileged time of social and political stability with only a hint of unrest, as when Socrates tells of the political abuses of the democracy's Council and of the Thirty Tyrants which succeeded them. There were destabilizing political and social issues in ancient Athens, but we rarely see them directly in Plato's dialogues.

Foremost of these issues must have been war and security. For the 150 years from the successful defeat of the Persian invasions to the conquest by Macedonia, the Greek city-states, especially the largest, Athens, Sparta and later Thebes, were at war with each other. The cities united to repulse the Persians in 490 and 480 but had no reason to remain together except common defense. Persian policy thereafter changed from one of direct attack to one of playing off the Greek cities against each other so that they would be too weak to attack Persia itself. The separate ambitions of Athens and Sparta were encouraged or hindered by Persia but would have been adequate to disrupt Greek affairs without any foreign interference.

Almost from the moment they were united in the struggle to save Greece itself, Athens and Sparta viewed each other with suspicion. Sparta already had the strongest army, with a well-developed culture and system of allies to maintain it. Athens developed its sea power during the wars with Persia, especially when it continued by itself the liberation of the islands and towns of Asia Minor known as Ionia. These coastal cities became the foundation of Athen's allies and increasingly her empire. The next fifty years were a period of explosive growth and accumulation of wealth in Athens, especially the later years under the direction of Pericles when the Acropolis, which had been destroyed in the Persian War, was rebuilt. This Golden Age of Athens with its flowering of the arts, its wide commerce in goods and ideas, and its development of a refined, democratic and comfortable yet not sumptuous life for its citizens contrasted sharply with the conservative clinging to the traditional cultural institutions of Sparta. Here the main value was military preparedness, with men and women living in separate barracks much of the time, the accumulation of wealth expressly prohibited and the duplication of the past serving as the standard in the arts.

After decades of jockeying for position, undermining each other's allies and pursuing every strategic advantage in an endless series of small regional wars, in 431 Athens and Sparta finally began their war of mutual destruction, the Peloponnesian War, named after the southern peninsula of Greece where Sparta is located. The war ended 27 years later with Athens defeated and both sides so exhausted that neither could reestablish its empire or its hegemony over the rest of Greece. The next sixty years continued the pattern of smaller regional wars, with Thebes rising as a third major power. Then in 338 after trying to unite their cities peacefully, Philip of Macedonia united the Greeks under his army. During the 150 years from the first Persian invasion, there was not a single decade of peace for the citizens of Athens.

When Plato was writing in the twilight of the Athenian Empire, popular belief revered two heroic ages in the past, when gods and humans seemed to live closer together and perhaps be more similar. 800 years earlier the Trojan War produced the mythical heroes Achilles,

Odysseus and others who set the epic standards for strength and cunning for all of Greece. 100 years earlier the heroes of Marathon and other battles against the Persians set a more human standard and led Athens into eighty years of prosperity. Then while the Peloponnesian War was raging, full of its own heroes and scoundrels, a different type of hero's battles were chronicled, another golden age when the gods spoke more directly to humans. Socrates was elevated as a hero against the socially destructive forces of sophistry and rhetoric.

Greek Education: Sophistry replaces Traditional Values

In the funeral speech quoted by Thucydides, Pericles calls Athens the school of Greece. It was the center for the development, criticism and consumption of new ideas. Its democracy supported a freedom of expression limited only by one's ability to defend one's self in court. Aristophanes in his comedies not only refers to or acts out on the stage most bodily functions, but also skewers most of the well-known celebrities in Athens, including Socrates whom he attacks for being a sophist. Sophistry is a major theme in Plato's dialogues. Three famous sophists (Protagoras, Gorgias and Hippias) and one sophistic scoundrel (Euthydemus) lend their names to dialogues, while the job title itself names another. The problem of how to distinguish sophistry from philosophy, the problem which Socrates addresses first in the *Apology* before he can even begin his defense, is examined in almost half of the dialogues and will be addressed in the following section on rhetoric. At this point we need to review some intellectual history for which the term *sophistes* will serve as a convenient reference point.

From Homer through the sixth century the term refers to wise people who know the meaning of life and how to live it, such as the revered seven Sages. It is generally linked to traditional values. By the fifth century it has taken on an additional meaning of one who has know-how or skill in some practical area or craft. As skill areas develop their own values, requiring *sophia*, their relation to traditional values becomes less fixed. Efficiency and success, as we see in our present culture, become their own values.

Later in the fifth century a group of men, assuming the "sophist" name, initiate a new vocation, offering to teach for a fee whatever audiences wanted to learn and were willing to pay for. Hippias in the shorter dialogue with his name is more outspoken than others in his self-promotion but the breadth of his claimed areas of expertise gives a good idea of what the sophists offered. Here is Socrates recounting Hippias' accomplishments.

> You are the wisest of people in the greatest number of crafts, as I once heard you boasting...You once went to Olympia with everything you had on your body the product of your own work... the ring you were wearing... And another signet, too, was your work, and a strigil and an oil bottle... you had cut from leather the sandals you were wearing and had woven your cloak and tunic. And what seemed to everyone most unusual and an exhibition of the greatest wisdom was when you said that the belt you wore around your tunic was like the very expensive Persian ones... you brought poems with you--epic, tragic and dithyrambs, and many writings of all sorts in prose. You said you came with knowledge that distinguished you from all others on the subjects we have been discussing (arithmetic, geometry, astronomy), and also about rhythm, and harmony, and the correctness of letters... and your artful technique of memory, in which you think you are most brilliant. (368b-e)

The main learning that the audiences wanted, especially the young men with money and political prospects, were the most desirable social and political skills: literary interpretation, political science, and especially public speaking or rhetoric. Such education previously was handed down through families or friends for the good of these groups and the city as a whole, but it was never bought by an individual for personal gain. The sophists' practical realism in approaching the problem of creating a persuasive speech resulted in preferring believability over truth. With this approach, traditional values became merely opportunities for manipulation. The honor arising from public values and support is replaced by the self-confidence, cunning, and even deceit of the opportunist. The term "sophistry" now becomes ambivalently charged. To call someone a sophist is pejorative, referring to his too clever arguments which charm and deceive without regard for the truth and his concern for his own interests, especially income, over those of the *polis*. Yet the ability to use sophistic winning arguments is highly valued, especially by the youth who see this as a sure means to success. Socrates' young friend Hippocrates in the *Protagoras* blushes when Socrates suggests that he may become a sophist if trained by one, yet he still goes eagerly to learn the tricks of persuasive speech (312a).

This evolution of the term *sophistes* reflects significant changes in Greek culture. Since the year 1200, the divinely inspired oral performances of the many Trojan War epics served as scriptural authority much as the *Bible* does for Christians. Around 800 Homer created a version of the *Iliad* and the *Odyssey* which became standard and was written down some 200 years later. These continued as the foundation of Greek education for at least another 200 years. In the oral culture, these stories were repeated so many times that people would memorize and be able to repeat large sections of the text. The singer of the story would memorize the entire poem for a performance lasting, perhaps, four hours a night for six nights. We still have such abilities, as with young children who after several nights of listening are able to correct any deviations in the parent's telling or my students who have seen a certain movie dozens of times and can now repeat the entire dialogue.

Plato's dialogues with their similar interweaving of stories and arguments build upon the tradition of Homer and especially its fifth century evolution in the development of theater and tragedy as a focus for the discussion, criticism and resolution of social problems and values. The theater occurring at the festival of Dionysus continued the religious context of divinely inspired literature. The words of Aeschylus and Sophocles could be quoted, as Phaedrus does in the *Symposium*, to present the authority of traditional values, much as the *Bible* is quoted. But the ancient stories being retold by these writers have an increasingly personal edge to them. They are being used for persuasion, as, for example, in Aeschylus' support of nationalism or Euripides' later criticism of it. The traditional stories from the old oral epics whose meaning underpinned Greek culture were now being manipulated to serve the purposes of the poets. Euripides intentionally develops the character of Medea in his play to be a sympathetic person in opposition to her duplicitous Greek lover Jason, thus challenging the audience's expected Greek superiority over the barbarians.

The words of Homer seemed to be available in their literal truth to his audience, and once the story was known after many hearings, these words would be commonly understood by everyone. There was no personal authorship in motive or meaning. The story, again like the *Bible*, somehow had its own integrity and transparency. Increasingly the use of plots by the poets, like that of arguments by the sophists, seemed to serve plausibility and public opinion rather than the truth, or at least required some interpretation in order to be understood.

The last element in this move away from simple traditional values is the cultural relativism arising from Greek contact with her neighbors, especially Persia, and more contact between the cities themselves. Before the fifth century each city had its own patron gods and religious festivals, its own constitution and army, and its own history and future. The Persian Wars began to unravel the cocoons within which the separate cities had been able to develop. Here the various cities had united their armies to fight together under a more or less unified command, although someone, usually Sparta, was always threatening to take their army home. Military technique became less a matter of local tradition than of efficiency. More important, as the two great alliance systems of Athens and Sparta spread, cities were encouraged to adopt a democratic constitution like Athens or an oligarchic one like Sparta. Each city developed well-organized factions supporting these two causes, the poor siding with Athens and freedom, the rich siding with Sparta and strict law and order protecting property. As the internal wars developed during the century, cities became less distinctive (and in some cases completely disappeared as punishment for insurrection) as they united or revolted between and sometimes beyond the two alliances. Athens became distinctive for retaining the fewest distinctions. It became a city of the world, cosmopolitan, accepting resident aliens from all of greater Greece to live in the port area called the Piraeus, with their new customs, ideas and industry and permitting them broad freedom to continue their customs, like the religious festival of Bendis in Piraeus, which frames the action in the *Republic*.

As the cities came in more contact and competition, the question of which customs were the best naturally arose. Should you exercise naked (gymnasium means a place to train naked) or clothed, have elected juries or appointed or selected by lot, swear by Zeus, Apollo or Poseidon? Herodotus wrote a history of the Persian Wars and of his travels around Persia, Egypt and greater Greece. He frequently marvels at but accepts as true the strange customs of his distant neighbors. In one famous example, the Persian king Darius points out that Greeks who burn their dead are equally repulsed by the idea of eating them as an Indian peoples who normally eat their dead are repulsed by the idea of burning them. In order to evaluate the customs of any culture, one must use a system of values based upon some specific culture. It seemed there could be no culturally-free evaluations. Then nature was introduced as a separate source of value into this debate.

Nature had been developing as an independent entity for the last hundred years. Before this nature was an expression of the gods. It was divided up among them and reflected their state of satisfaction. If they were pleased, it flourished, and if they were not, it did not. Nature was wholly dependent, and if one wanted something of nature, such as a good harvest, the way to accomplish this was through making sure that the proper god was satisfied. Then nature began to be considered as something in its own right. Thales (624-545) began to wonder about the structure and order (*cosmos*) in nature, if everything were composed of one basic stuff. His candidate was water, which encompassed three of the four known elements: earth (ice as solid), air (steam as gas), water, and only fire could not clearly be derived. Anaximenes (580-500) chose air, which does cover all four, with fiery lightning falling from the sky, as well as liquid water and solid snow and ice. The particular solutions of these early naturalists were not as important as the fact that they were studying nature in the first place. Nature could be studied and an account (*logos*) be given of it. For this to be true, nature had to have some stability apart from the caprice of the gods, similar to our 17th century problem of freeing nature from God's miracles in order to make it a stable object of inquiry.

An independent nature (*phusis*) becomes available as a culturally neutral means for describing the world, including human cultures (*nomos*) and values, and even becomes a value in its own right. Acting in concert with the regularities of nature becomes one of the means to living well. Thus in early medicine certain plants cure or sicken regardless of cultural background. But as a universal and stable nature replaced the arbitrary traditions of culture as the model for human behavior, a great controversy arose with the Sophists as the champions of nature. Traditional belief thought it was the business of civilization to raise humans above the level of the beasts, while the new thinking held that human nature was as much a part of nature as any other living thing.

"The advantage of the stronger" seemed to be the rule everywhere in nature, and so the development of power over each other appeared to be the natural way for humans to behave. When Meno in his dialogue finally gives a simple definition of human virtue, it is the possession of power to secure good things (78c). The *Euthydemus* examines this idea of "the stronger" with two ex-wrestling coaches who have now taken up the easier vocation of coaching wrestling with words. A person is stronger if she can make moves with words, just as with bodies, which maneuver an opponent into a compromised position and defeat. Being clever is a type of human strength, and Sophists teach cleverness.

A problem, however, with having power and being able to get one's way is whether what one thinks is to one's advantage actually is. Do I know what is beneficial to me or could I be mistaken? The same Meno who wanted to possess power did achieve it as a general in an expedition against Persia. He was off to accumulate the riches of this empire but instead was captured and tortured to death. Socrates examines this notion of one's advantage with Thrasymachus in the first book of the *Republic*. Is one's advantage what one thinks it is or is there some objective way to determine what it really is? The stronger one is, the more dangerous it is to pursue one's advantage if one is mistaken about what is truly beneficial. The advantage of a strong animal is that it can reproduce and maintain its genes. But with humans it is more complicated. Would someone with a fatal genetic disease want to produce children doomed to suffering and premature death? Sophists encouraged their audience to believe that we each know what is good for us, that the audience could judge the goodness of the sophists. Philosophy will use our ignorance as to our own good as one of its organizing principles and fundamental problems.

Traditional values in the individual Greek cities were weakened after the year 500 by contact and competition with both other Greek cities and other cultures, by the appearance of new problems outside the traditional framework, such as military alliances, by the change in art from expressing Muse-inspired divine truth to artists expressing their own beliefs, and by the rise of inquiry into nature and a corresponding evolution in religious belief from gods as supernatural magicians into representatives of natural forces. (In the *Phaedrus* the god Boreas is merely a wind.) There arose a personal and social need for a new source of values, and into this vacuum stepped both rhetoric, as the means to effectively discuss and persuade about values or any other topic, and philosophy, as the means to inquire about values or any other topic. We are now ready to examine rhetoric more carefully.

Rhetoric - Part I

Speeches were an important part of Greek life, especially in Athens. The Homeric heroes were renown for being "doers of deeds and speakers of words." The powerful slayer of men Achilles is matched with the devious teller of tales Odysseus as role models. This devious aspect is known to us in Odysseus' repeated use of disguises and false autobiographies in the *Odyssey* and his most famous trick in creating the Trojan Horse. This lead to the proverb "Beware of Greeks bearing gifts," but it could just as easily have been "Beware of Greeks telling stories."

When Herodotus describes his adventures and the progress of the Persian War, he provides recreations of the words people used in their addresses, arguments and discussions. Thucydides does this even more in his history of the Peloponnesian War, recreating political debates in which each side expresses its position in a speech, while the narrative records the results and the political consequences. He also recreates individual display speeches, like Pericles' funeral oration for slain Athenian soldiers in which he glorified Athens and its way of life.[4]

The point of interest in all these speeches is believability and its relation to truth. The concern with plausibility gives rise to the study of rhetoric, while that with truth gives rise to philosophy. Both develop during the fifth century. In this chapter we will discuss the background of rhetoric's development and social role, which will prepare us to return to this topic at the end of the next chapter after we have examined philosophy. Then we will be able to determine whether the two really do differ and how.

Facts of Greek political life lead to the need for individual citizens to be able to make speeches, as well as the legendary and historical heroes. In the democracies in Athens and elsewhere, large public assemblies debated issues and voted their resolutions. Effective speakers guided their fellow citizens in developing a line of argument to support or reject government initiatives such as war, commerce, public construction, and foreign affairs, much as in our times. Political power depended upon effective speaking. Good ideas also helped, but if they could not be expressed in simple terms, the public assembly had little specialized training or patience. Even more to our point, an effective speaker can take a mediocre idea and make it sound great. Political power resides in the ability to maintain popular support, not in having the best ideas. Demosthenes, for example, successfully convinced the Athenian assembly to resist the overtures of Philip of Macedon, which lead to an unnecessary war and defeat for the city.

The traditional Greek definition of personal success was to live a good and satisfying life. Political success likewise resulted in a satisfying civic life. Stories like *Oedipus* showed the fragility and complexity of this happiness. To sound like one knows what one is talking about and knows how to attain this, however, may require only a simple study of what the audience knows about an issue and wants to hear. Meno in his dialogue has learned "to give a bold and grand answer to any question you may be asked, as experts are likely to do." If he acts confidently and sounds like an expert, people will believe he knows what he is talking about. This enables him to accomplish what the sophists commonly promised the crowds they were courting for business. "He himself was ready to answer any Greek who wished to question him, and every question was answered" (70b-c).[5]

25

Today public opinion polls guide our society's debates and help politicians to "sound like an expert" because they identify the terms in which the audience is ready to receive whatever information is offered. A clever politician will use them to prey upon the public's desires and fears, not seeking to foster any understanding of an issue so much as to accumulate power for themselves. Such political hopefuls in Greece turned to the study of rhetoric as the skill of matching a style of speaking with the particular beliefs of any audience.

The second relevant fact of Athenian life was the legal system. Individuals had to make their own cases in court, either as prosecutors or defendants. There was no legal apparatus, as today, with government officials to arrest suspects and to present in court the case against them. Criminal cases were brought by one citizen against another. An effective speaker could harass his enemies by bringing false suits and then arguing persuasively or could commit crimes calculating that he could overcome any potential prosecutor's speech. This is the picture Callicles draws in the *Gorgias* to convince Socrates to pursue rhetoric instead of philosophy.

> If anyone were to arrest you or any of your kind and drag you off to prison, declaring that you'd broken the law though you hadn't done a thing, you know perfectly well that you wouldn't be able to help yourself. You'd stand there, reeling and gaping and not have a thing to say. If the fellow hales you into court, though his accusations are never so unproven and false, you'll die the death if he chooses to claim the death penalty. (486b)

This, of course, echoes the situation in the *Apology* where Socrates is being prosecuted for political reasons. Socrates does respond to Callicles that when it counts before the court of truth, it will be he who will be at a loss for words and doomed to die. Whether Socrates adequately defends himself and his vocation will be examined further in the next chapter.

The Sophists, as we have seen, taught a variety of subjects, but none was in greater demand than rhetoric. In the *Protagoras* when Socrates and his young friend Hippocrates arrive at the sophists' residence, they find Hippias talking about physics and astronomy, Prodicus clarifying the fine distinctions between words with similar meanings and Protagoras answering any question on any subject. But when the conversation turns to the art of politics and rhetoric's role, they all participate and defend this central teaching. This is their bread and butter. In order to sound convincing, one needs to know a little about a lot, so the sophists were polymaths, with vocabularies and theoretical simplifications extending into almost every area of human experience. They did not teach one how to converse with, much less to practice the vocation of, a general or shipbuilder or medical doctor, but rather how to converse on these topics with an audience largely ignorant of the actual methods and practices of these specialists.[6]

That a politician should know a little about a lot seems beneficial for someone who needs to make informed decisions and at least know when to seek more information and whom to ask. Here the modern supporters of the sophists rightly defend their role in developing the more broadly informed and flexible citizenry which democracy requires. Yet the same broad but shallow knowledge can be used to manipulate an audience which knows less and to keep them ignorant. A major difference between philosophy and rhetoric is that philosophy seeks to open up inquiry and expand knowledge, while rhetoric seeks to close inquiry and limit knowledge so that it can maintain most people in ignorance, making them a stable and controllable audience.

One problem with the art of persuasion is that it has no necessary relationship to the truth. What is said is determined by what will be believed. Once rhetoric with its use of lying is introduced into a conversation or culture, it is very difficult to detect it or eradicate it. Lying only works within a system that expects the truth. If lying is expected, the language will be discounted or discarded. Thus rhetoric can sustain itself only by hiding what it is doing, as in Socrates' claim not to be a good speaker in the *Apology*, Pausanias' claim to have merely improvised his speech in the *Symposium* or Socrates' hiding his head while he delivers his rhetorical speech in the *Phaedrus*. The need for rhetoric to conceal itself from others can become even more vicious when we conceal it from ourselves. Sometimes our own lies are raised to consciousness yet we prefer to ignore them, as when Jocasta advises Oedipus not to question the shepherd about any infants left out on the hillsides to die. She has convinced herself not to think about the consequences of this past act of hers. Oedipus insists on the inquiry, thus exposing Jocasta's rhetoric to herself. Her shame from the incest she can no longer hide drives her to suicide. The problems of such self-deception as well as the deception of others will enter into our later discussion of the philosophical rehabilitation of rhetoric.

Religion

Some discussion of religious beliefs and practices in Greece and Athens is needed before we begin reading the dialogues, especially since some commentators use Plato's membership in a particular religious group to explain his use of certain images or arguments and his need to prove certain ideas, such as the immortality of the soul. It is not known that Plato belonged to any religious group, so once again, the arguments *to* his religious beliefs are interesting and often possible, though by no means necessary, while the arguments *from* his religious beliefs are almost always without any sure basis and usually only derive from the previous conjectures about his beliefs in the first place.

By the year 400 religious belief in Athens resembled somewhat the variety of religious belief and non-belief in the United States today. Some held to the traditional beliefs in the Homeric Olympian gods. Some reformed these beliefs to be less superstitious and more rational and moral. Some followed newer, often imported religious movements such as the Orphic and other Mystery cults. And some denied the existence of the gods or at least any gods that we can claim to know of.

Traditional beliefs were both national and local. Each city had its own nature deities (rivers, trees, caves) and local hero cults. Phaedrus in his dialogue follows this when, debating which god to choose as guarantor of his oath, he selects a nearby tree (236d). Each city also had its own specializations of the Olympic gods. Athena in Athens, Poseidon in Sparta, Hera in Argos were the special patrons and protectors of these cities but resumed their normal functions elsewhere. Gods could be worshipped under more than one guise, as Pausanias makes use of in his *Symposium* speech. Athens has two temples to Aphrodite, one a local cult with possible connections to the city's courtesans and the other an older tradition, possibly from Syria.

Traditional religious beliefs also had political standing. Religious festivals, like the theater festival of Dionysus, were an official part of city life and civic holidays. To be a citizen of a city included the responsibility to respect its gods. Such laws were usually not strictly enforced except in times of political stress, as when the newly returned democratic government, in their attempt to rid Athens of destabilizing elements, prosecuted Socrates for impiety. More typical of the religious climate is such a figure as Euthyphro, a religious zealot, who by his own admission most people did not take seriously.

New religious beliefs mostly came from eastern barbarian lands and gradually assimilated through the eastern and northern Greek cities. Thus the resident aliens from Thrace brought their goddess Bendis to the Piraeus in Athens and to the *Republic*. More important was the earlier introduction of the enthusiastic (being divinely possessed) and orgiastic (loss of self-identity in the fervor of group celebrations) worship of Dionysus, a wild uncivilized god of intoxication and reincarnation. The Orphics were one branch of Dionysus worshippers whose beliefs echo many elements from Plato's dialogues. Humans are of mixed divine and earthly origin, created by the blood of the slain Dionysus who was later resurrected and the ashes of the Titans who once ruled the earth. Our divine souls are captive in bodily prisons and can be freed by following the ascetic way of Orphic life through several cycles of reincarnation and then initiation into the orgies of Dionysus in order to become free. The final satisfaction in life is not in this world which is only a test of our readiness for the next one.

Orphism built upon the earlier beliefs of the Eleusinian Mysteries, mentioned in the *Meno*, that humans could prepare in this life for a better life hereafter. Orphism influenced Pythagoras who was known for his research in mathematics and astronomy as well as founding a strict religious brotherhood. He believed, like the Orphics, in the denial of bodily desires so that the soul could be purified and attain ever more complete reincarnations until it finally achieved freedom of the restrictions of the material world. The story of the *Phaedo* is retold among Pythagoreans, with many themes of their beliefs woven throughout, but whether Plato is supporting them or criticizing them is an open question.

Among those with some learning, scientific inquiry had circumscribed the arena of divine activity and driven it from most daily affairs. As Aristotle said, rocks are consistently downward tending due to their nature and not just episodically so by divine direction. Yet the credulous, then as now, continued to believe that the gods were involved in the minutiae of our lives and could be cajoled to end a sickness, attract a lover, or stop a careening chariot. Sophisticated Athenians knew arguments for the earth being round, that the sun's motion across the sky was only apparent and that natural phenomena, such as rainbows or lightning, did not require the gods for their occurrence.

Many of these arguments against the senselessness of supernatural explanations began with Xenophanes (570-470) and created the underpinnings for later atheism and agnosticism. He attacked then current conceptions of the gods on several fronts. Using the gods to explain natural phenomena destroyed the possibility of our ever being able to understand them and use them to improve our lives.

Belief in the gods interferes with our efforts to take care of ourselves. Also the amorality of the gods' reported sexual and social activities were acceptable in so far as they represented forces of nature, but as they became more identified with human beings, they were taken as models for human behavior. Their sexual assaults and flings now looked decidedly immoral and unacceptable for truly divine beings. Either the stories were wrong or these were not true gods. Finally, Xenophanes drew out the consequences for religion of cultural relativism and saw that we humans make our gods in our own image, with people from various climates each thinking that the gods resemble their own physical features. He even pushed this further.

> But if cattle and horses or lions had hands, or were able to draw with their hands and do the works that men can do, horses would draw the forms of the gods like horses, and cattle like cattle, and they would make their bodies such as they each had themselves.[7]

The gods we imagine are merely idealized projections of ourselves. If there are gods, why should they have human shape or any shape at all? Do they offer us direction or confusion in guiding our behavior? Are they organizational principles in nature or obstructions? Such questions were part of the fifth century discussions about religion. They evoke a culture where the trial and execution of Socrates was more like the political witch-hunts of our McCarthy era than those of the rigorously orthodox Puritans in Massachusetts.

This review of fifth and fourth century Athenian culture has examined those aspects that have some connection with Plato's dialogues, both the environments in which the discussions occur and the topics discussed. The presentation here has been very general. If successful, it has given readers some idea of the many dimensions involved in understanding an author and his writings, alike in ancient Athens and today, and some of the threads to follow when these topics come up in Plato's dialogues, to which we will now turn.

Notes

1. J.H. Randall, *Plato: Dramatist of the Life of Reason* (New York: Columbia University Press, 1970) 36.
2. A. E. Taylor, *Plato* (New York: Meridian, 1956) 8.
3. L. A. Post, *Thirteen Epistles of Plato* (1925), 25. Quoted in J. E. Raven, *Plato's Thought in the Making* (Cambridge: Cambridge University Press, 1965), 22.
4. There was an annual "Memorial Day" in Athens to honor those fallen in battle for the *polis*, with a contest to select the speaker for the celebration. In Plato's *Menexenus* Socrates gives an overblown rendition of such a speech which he says he learned from Pericles' mistress Aspasia, whom he says also authored Pericles' speech.
5. Compare *Hippias Minor* 363d and *Gorgias* 448d.
6. A famous television commercial began "I'm not a real doctor but I play one on TV." It persuaded us by assuming that the TV character fulfilled the audience's stereotype of a doctor better than a real one would. The audience would thus listen more to their own presumption of what such an expert should be than to a real one.
7. Kirk and Raven, The Presocratic Philosophers (Cambridge: Cambridge University Press, 1971), 169.

2

Philosophy

When reading the works of an important thinker, look first for
the apparent absurdities in the text and ask yourself how a
sensible person could have written them. When you find an
answer,... when these passages make sense, then you may
find that the more central passages, ones you previously
thought you understood, have changed their meaning.
                                        - Thomas Kuhn[1]

One of the liveliest controversies within philosophy concerns the
nature of philosophy itself. Philosophers describe what they are doing
in many of ways: determining the rules for proper thinking, behavior
and feeling (logic, ethics and aesthetics), creating a habit of rational
response to the stimuli of our environment, sanitizing language and the
ideas it describes by eliminating unnecessary or even dangerous confusions, justifying the ways of god to humans or the ways of faith to reason, etc. For some generations the understanding of metaphysics, the
basic principles of existence, was the highest calling, while for our
times metaphysics has become synonymous with the occult both in
bookstores and at "psychic" demonstrations. Are these differences
mainly disagreements over changing vocabulary, while the nature of
philosophy remains mostly constant, or does this activity itself change?

In order to understand Plato's philosophic writings, we must begin with some clarification of what he means by philosophy, but how to do this seems to beg some question no matter how we proceed. Let's assume that philosophy is the understanding and practice of proper reasoning, then may a philosopher ever intentionally use a fallacy without warning us? When fallacies appear in the dialogues, is Plato then doing something other than philosophy? Or if we join Ockham in preferring the minimum number of explanatory principles, then do we fault Plato when he brings in the gods to explain the cause of virtue or a whole heavenly apparatus to explain the origin of our ideas?

Most contemporary philosophy rejects any attempt to construct a rational system offering a complete explanation of human experience, and yet Plato seems to do this with his description of the Ideal City in the *Republic*, the vision of the Ideal Forms in the *Phaedrus*, the explanation of the eternal life of the soul in the *Phaedo*, and so on. Many commentators and textbooks begin with the assumption that Plato must have been building the very sort of system it is their philosophical responsibility to expose and reject. This puts our conception of Plato in conflict with our conception of philosophy itself. Our investment in our idea of philosophy is the greater and less likely to change, so that we set up Plato as a foil. We show our superiority by exposing the alleged shortcomings of his City, Forms and Immortality. We are pleased when our power has knocked down the straw man.

I believe the arguments in the dialogues usually can be knocked down. In our litigious, competitive, eristic culture, so similar to ancient Athens, this is most often the end of the matter. But for Plato I believe that this is exactly the beginning. Philosophy concerns both the destruction and construction of arguments and ideas, that is, with their criticism. The absurdities we find in a thinker's work may be just those places where our self-confidence is defending us from examining problematic areas of our own lives and ideas. Plato might not present so much a system of answers as one of helping us to ask questions.[2] No matter what our philosophic point of departure, Kuhn's warning must remain in our ears. If we encounter absurdities when reading a recognized philosopher, we must first examine whether our own concept of philosophy and its method is flexible enough to incorporate whatever insight may be lurking within these absurd–sounding statements. Our desire to be right must be tempered by the dangers of being wrong.

Plato has Socrates compare philosophy with dying and elaborate this with all sorts of embarrassing talk about the soul, its health, immortality, reincarnation, and stories about what life is like in the afterworld. He also proposes that philosophers should be kings, admits that he really knows nothing (except about love), states that he spends all of his time examining himself, denies that he is an accomplished speaker while managing to control every discussion except his own trial where his life is a stake, and more. These are all strange statements, and the goal of what follows is to develop a notion of philosophy expansive enough to make sense of all of them. I hope that the previous chapter established more similarities than differences between Plato's time and our own. I will suggest that the issues that bother us today as philosophers also bothered Plato, and that our notions of current philosophical correctness often ride uneasily upon Plato's apparent absurdities. What seems so unphilosophical may be exactly the places we need to examine in order to better understand the procedures and purposes of Plato's philosophy.

I. Death

The place to begin our discussion is rather arbitrary. There are many threads that, if we consistently use our reason to unravel and follow any one of them, will teach us something about the nature of philosophy. This is one reason why Plato wrote so many dialogues, to present different means of access into the philosophic life. Among these multiple dimensions to our lives and thoughts, no single thread provides the ultimate means of access. Descartes for his *Meditations* removes himself from life as much as possible in order to find such a thread, while Plato's action always occurs in the middle of things. There are removals to the edges of life's confusions: the shelter of homes, the isolation of a prison, the open space outside the city's walls, but there is always contact with other people and their activities. Thus in what follows, while trying to follow the thread of death, other threads will weave themselves around our theme. Our reward for tolerating this awkward organization is a better chance to appreciate the whole cloth of Plato's writings.

In the *Phaedo* Socrates describes philosophy as "the practice of dying and being dead" (64a). Since he does die here, these words gain a certain pleasing literalness, yet dying seems to be something that you can practice only while you are alive and accomplish only once. The character of Socrates somehow occupies both of these spaces. For the readers of the dialogues, the historical Socrates is dead, and his last ideas seem as fixed and unchanging as the dead tailor's last cloak in Cebes' story in the *Phaedo* (87b-e). The dramatic Socrates, however, is

34

alive and his ideas still subject to change. Is he practicing being dead in order to become as rigid in his thought as his body will be in death? When asked how he would like to be buried, he laughs, "Anyway you like, if you can catch me and I do not escape you" (115c). The death of the body might not provide the final closure of a person's ideas as suggested above; Socrates is still on the run. His body's death will not provide us with the occasion for a comparable morgue photograph of how his last ideas looked. If it is not the fixity that seems to accompany death that Socrates desires, then what does he want? What is it that he is practicing?

To understand this puzzle, as the *Phaedo* makes clear, one has to understand the immortal nature of our *psuche*, the Greek word most commonly translated as "soul." This word developed three meanings as it evolved, and all are relevant for us. Originally it meant the force which caused something to have life in it. This idea comes into English though the parallel Latin word "*anima*", whose presence in a thing makes it *anima*ted or able to move itself, as *anima*ls do. When a soldier died in Homer's story of the Trojan War, his soul always had to escape from his dying body, because life could not be present where there was death.[3] The second meaning of *psuche* as "spirit", our common meaning of "soul", developed as religious thought elaborated how the life force lived on in the afterworld of Hades. The sullen, speechless shades of the Homeric poems evolve into beings that are rewarded, punished and reincarnated. The life force takes on a life. The third meaning describes what is most lively within us as human beings, what does not sleep when the body does--the mind. Socrates plays back and forth between these meanings, frequently using the religious vocabulary and imagery connected with the life of the soul to help us understand the less well-known life of the mind.

An ascetic person could practice the death of the body in order to better appreciate the life of the disembodied spirit. The philosopher practices the death of her ideas in order to better appreciate the life of the mind. This sounds paradoxical at first. Why should we need to do anything special in order to appreciate the element that is most lively within us? Because we spend most of our lives trying to think as little as possible. What makes Socrates such an odd character is that he thinks so much, just as his partners in the dialogues are noteworthy for their avoidance, whenever possible, of any heavy thinking.

Since some thinking goes on all the time, the distinction here is one of quality. Most of our thinking is not philosophical but rather calculative. We are in situations where we have to decide what to do next. We think we know our options and how to evaluate them. We have a formula for how to proceed, punch in the appropriate data, and come up with an answer giving us a clear direction to follow. Much of this calculating does not even reach the level of consciousness, as we go through most of our daily activities in a semi-habitual routine.

Philosophic thinking, on the other hand, occurs when we have a problem and are not even sure what exactly is wrong or which formula to apply. Socrates' repeated efforts to define the main Greek *aretai* or virtues: justice, piety, courage, moderation and wisdom, are examples of such thinking. This common translation of the Greek term *arete* as "virtue" can be misleading, and "excellence" or even "success" may serve us better. Many people, often following Aristotle's comments on the historical Socrates,[4] think that the character Socrates has some narrow moral concern here, whereas the issue is the nature of human *excellence* in all its aspects and ambiguities. When Meno in his dialogue asks how to obtain *arete*, it is similar to a modern college student asking how to be successful in life, and it is similarly difficult to answer. Whom should I marry, what major should I select, what career should I follow, how many children, if any, should I have? Although these are all "should" questions, they do not seem to be ethical in our current use of this term. These are quality of life questions; how do I avoid getting myself in a mess, or, to use the ancient Greek perspective, how do I make myself happy. The Greeks repeatedly listened to stories about Oedipus, Agamemnon, Orestes, Priam, Achilles, stories about how difficult it is to do the right things to create whole, meaningful and satisfying lives.[5]

The *Meno* provides us with a good statement of this problem and some rich imagery in the discussion of how to solve it. Meno is a young man with those natural abilities that serve us well in early life. Like the Homeric heroes, he is able to physically excel and to speak well. Like many high school or college athletes, he is used to succeeding. Then his life takes on a greater scope as he moves out from his rural homeland, first to the big city of Athens and then to the world of Persia and beyond. In his conversation with Socrates, he is pausing to make sure he is on the right track. But like us when we similarly pause, he does not want to dig too deep. He wants assurance that he is doing the right thing but does not really want to examine all of his options. He will agree to calculate, hence the attraction of the geometry problem, but he is reluctant to think.

When Meno questions how we attain human excellence and success, he thinks three possibilities exhaust the responses, each of which he thinks he can also fulfill. Is it an inherited trait or a know-how to be taught or the result of some training? As he hangs out with the aristocrats in his hometown, he feels he shares their inheritance of the best human traits. Gorgias taught him rhetoric, the highest science, so he can sound like an expert in any field. And his training has made him sound in body and mind. He seems to have all the bases covered, but Socrates eliminates them all. He points out that excellent parents often have mediocre children, so it cannot be in the blood. Rich parents who can afford to train their children in all schools of practice also often have mediocre children. This leaves teaching, but they can find no teachers of excellence. Such a teacher would have to know what human excellence was and be able to transfer this knowledge to another. Both Socrates and Gorgias admit they cannot do this.

Having exhausted the three options, Socrates introduces a fourth, that the gods are really responsible when human excellence occurs. Meno readily agrees. He does not question whether the gods democratically distribute the potential for virtue to all or fate only their favorites to embody this excellence. He assumes he is a favored child of fate, as he has risen rapidly in the esteem of his fellows, becoming a general in his early twenties. He will soon leave Athens as one of the leaders of the Ten Thousand, a mercenary army ready to invade Persia and overthrow the Great King. If the gods distributed excellence, they must surely have given it to him. But fate is fickle, and it is dangerous to be yesterday's favorite. Meno marched his men into Persia only to be betrayed and captured along with his whole army. His fellow generals were killed in a trap, but he was saved to serve as a lesson for any future rebels against the King. Meno was tortured, slowly but steadily, over the course of a year and finally died. For a Greek audience his name evoked a strong image of human promise and failure.

Repeatedly in this dialogue Meno does not want to think but asks Socrates to give him the answers. This is Meno's notion of education. You pay for some piece of knowledge, and it is transferred to you. Socrates' notion, however, requires that the student be an active participant and ultimately finds the answers for herself. The scientific method uses the same approach where the learner directly experiences something in such a way that it convinces her that it is true. In science our participation in the experiment demonstrates to us the truth of the situation. Of course, such "truth" is limited by our ability to observe and our conception of what we think we are observing, but this is exactly the strength of the scientific method; it is self-consciously fallible and corrigible. Any experiment is only as true as the next time it is performed. The student, like the experimenter, does not accept the authority of any external expert, but rather proves to herself through the authority of her perceptions and reasoning. As these internal authorities are also fallible and corrigible, the seeker after knowledge regularly examines and tests her ideas and beliefs. And as we need others to test our experiments, so we need them to test our ideas.[6]

Socrates repeatedly tries to get Meno to examine his ideas for the same reason that any scientist would train her student, in order to improve the examination of ideas in general and more specifically the ideas of the teacher. Any good scientist would want her experiment, if faulty, to be proven faulty. There is no advantage to hanging on to falsehoods in science nor in philosophy. Socrates participates in these dialogues to articulate and criticize his own ideas and those of whoever will talk with him. He is trying to think and needs others to help overcome the efforts we all make to short-circuit this process: defensiveness, prejudice, haste, and lack of confidence. Much of his conversations are dedicated to dealing with these obstacles, and for this purpose the religious and death topics enter his talk with Meno.

In the first half of this dialogue, Socrates tries to get Meno to define *arete*. This is not Meno's interest here, but he does finally clarify that he thinks human excellence is having the power to get the goods in life. When Socrates bothers him further about how he knows which of the goods are really good, Meno is pushed to the brink of having to think and loses his patience. He insults Socrates by calling him a mind-numbing torpedo fish and then tries to block further inquiry by introducing the "learning paradox." How can one inquire into what he does not know, for either he already knows it and does not need to inquire or he does not know it and could never recognize it even if it were found (80 d-e). A crisis has been reached both in Meno's therapy, getting his soul healthy enough to engage in thinking, and for Socrates' hope of gaining a colleague in inquiry.

Socrates responds with a story about what other people have said about this. He takes himself out of the discussion, like any good therapist, and shifts the focus to an experience with which his partner can identify. The story tells the wisdom of the Mystery cults. "They say that the human soul is immortal; at times it comes to an end, which they call dying, at times it is reborn, but it is never destroyed, and one must therefore live one's life as piously as possible" (81b).

Socrates could have been an initiate and enthusiast in these cults, dancing in the orgies of the Orphic Dionysus or running with his pig to the sea at Eleusis,[7] but these images seem as incongruous here as the suggestion in the *Phaedo* that he was an all-knowing and authoritarian Pythagorean Master. The religious story enters not to focus on Socrates' ideas but to present neutral ideas and images, a territory where our ideas can be reworked outside the consequences of the real world, similar to play therapy with children.

Socrates' religious story here is not consistent with similar stories he tells in other dialogues.[8] Much ingenuity has been spent trying to save the systematic presentation of Socrates' ideas and of the Plato he is taken to represent. A cleaner explanation (remember Ockham) is that these stories are pedagogical and not autobiographical. They are tailored to the student's individual need at this moment. They do not offer final explanation but development of method. Meno needs a boost for his confidence if he is going to continue to participate in the inquiry. The story says a goddess takes the souls of human failures, punishes and purifies them and then forces them to live another life, somewhat similar to Socrates' treatment of Meno. Then from among this pitiful group arise some who will gain great mental and physical power and reputation. The key to this reversal of fortune is the time spent in Hades and the purification one experiences there, so that one may begin a new life with a clean record.

This reincarnation also provides "recollection" as Socrates calls it, access to the knowledge from all of one's previous lives.

> As the whole of nature is akin, and the soul has learned
> everything, nothing prevents a man, after recalling one thing
> only--a process men call learning--from discovering
> everything else for himself, if he is brave and does not tire of
> the search, for searching and learning are, as a whole,
> recollection. We must, therefore, not believe that debater's
> argument (the learning paradox), for it would make us idle,
> and fainthearted men like to hear it, whereas my argument
> makes them energetic and keen on the search. (81d-e)

Philosophy tries to explain rather than explaining away our experiences. If I am considering marriage, I might try to convince myself that this is the right choice by saying, as Aristophanes does in the *Symposium*, that somewhere in the world is the perfect mate for each of us, and this is my one and only. This ersatz explanation works only by eliminating the possibility of evidence and proof and thus of explanation itself. Plato's use of recollection operates in the same way. How do I know that whatever idea I have is the sure knowledge from my previous life and not just an opinion from this one? The story of recollection gives me hope that among my ideas there are some true ones, but it does not provide any labels. This story is just the sort to restore one's confidence for the search. It does not so much explain how knowledge is acquired as why we might be able to find it. As Socrates concludes, "I trust that this is true, and I want to inquire along with you into the nature of virtue" (81e). Note that even with recollection he does not *know* but can only *trust* that this is true, and that the result of the explanation is the return to further inquiry. Philosophy lives by inquiry, but to understand this life, we must further investigate death.

Earlier in the dialogue Socrates tells Meno that he should remain longer in Athens and be initiated into the Eleusinian Mysteries (76e). This is a simpler practice than that of the Orphics, without the reincarnation or Dionysian orgies. It offered a ceremonial encounter with death and the assurance that the soul survives in an afterworld. As a result of this experience, the initiates realize that they must care for their soul, as it will continue living after their body dies. There was no ongoing ritual or practice. Once the initiate had the death-type experience and subsequent realization, her life was forever changed.

Philosophy offers an experience with death similar to these initiations. For the religious Mysteries, the issue was the continued life of the soul after the death of the body. For the philosophic Mysteries the issue is the continued life of the mind after the death of a fundamental idea or opinion which provided significant support for one's life. Images from the Eleusinian Mysteries give us the confidence that if we are properly prepared, we can survive the death of a life-supporting idea. The Orphic and Pythagorean versions assure the continuing existence of the mind through its reincarnation in a succession of ideas.

The death scene in the *Phaedo* illustrates this usage. Socrates devotes this conversation on his last day to telling and examining stories about what we believe the next world to be like (61e). The stories he offers, with the exception of the closing myth of the soccer-ball shaped earth, are all arguments about ideas. The invisible world of the afterlife in Hades ("invisible" in Greek) is a useful religious image for discussing the invisible world of the soul life of our minds. Socrates here offers several interesting but not compelling arguments for one of these invisible inhabitants, the idea of the immortality of the soul. Note that his arguments are tailored to his audience, using Pythagorean reasoning with this largely Pythagorean group and causing the audience to observe some problems with their own style of thinking, just as he did with Meno's ideas of power. Socrates' arguments almost always have an *ad hominem* element, as we will examine further in the next chapter. This audience is as reluctant to harm Socrates' ideas due to the impending death of his body as to challenge their own ideas, and he finally drives them to stop nodding agreement to everything he says and to attack his statements.[9] When Simmias and Cebes hesitate to offer

40

their criticisms, Socrates receives their concern for his death with an encouraging laugh. (This is his laughingest dialogue.) Death here is something to be welcomed, and he encourages their counterarguments.[10] When they have stated their reasons for denying immortality, the audience is devastated.

> When we heard what they said we were all depressed, as we told each other afterwards. We had been quite convinced by the previous argument, and they seemed to confuse us again, and to drive us to doubt not only what had already been said but also what was going to be said, lest we be worthless critics or the subject itself admitted of no certainty. (88c)

Plato draws out this death scene with even the frame characters intruding to lament the passing of Socrates' arguments. Socrates goes so far as to propose a formal mourning for these arguments unless they can be brought back to life and reincarnated. He especially points out the vulnerability of the soul during this bereavement. "I am in danger at this moment of not having a philosophical attitude about this" (91a).

When a fundamental idea, one that we have used and relied upon, is brought to criticism and dies, we may lose faith in the possibility of *logos* itself, a complex word meaning language, speech, reasoning (logic), argument, explanation, account, proportion, and reasonable discourse itself.[11] The connected meanings of this key term reflect one of the main principles of Greek philosophy, that reason and speech must go together, that explanation must always be able to give an account of itself, as opposed to the supernatural and superrational.

The problem for *logos* here in the *Phaedo* is that after we developed, tested and believed an idea, such as the immortality of the soul, it turned out to be false. If we set out with the same method to try again, what better chance do we have of success? If we are offered reincarnation, why bother? As Socrates here discusses, there are two manifestations of this loss of faith, misology and eristic, passive and active. Misology, which Socrates calls the greatest of human evils, is the hatred of *logos* itself, the belief that no argument can ever be sound nor offer any reliable guidance in life. Eristic (from the Greek *eris* meaning strife) is the attitude of "the uneducated" toward *logos* (91a). For them argument is merely an opportunity for competition, for showing off one's power (similar to Meno) and not for the evaluation of the ideas discussed. They believe the clever use of rhetoric can reverse our opinions on any topic, and so do not expect discussion to provide any access to truth.

These are the dangers of living a rational life for which we have to prepare by practicing dying and being dead. We need to become more sensitive to the experience of how our ideas work: bringing our ideas to criticism, finding that an idea cannot explain what it pretends to, accepting the death of this idea and the subsequent hole in our understanding, passing through the dark night of the soul when no replacement ideas appear, and finally finding a new candidate. Then our soul has a better chance, not only of surviving, but of becoming stronger. It sounds like falling in and out of love: elation, suspicion, confusion, depression, reorganization, elation. In a significant sense, philosophy is the preparation for being depressed. When our world has crashed, when our career, lover, parenting, friends, etc. has failed us or we failed it, then we need to be prepared or face being crushed.

Modern psychological hygiene suggests diversifying our self image so that it has more than one support, toughening it by facing as many positive and negative experiences in a supportive environment as possible, and clarifying it by participating in meaningful discourse with a variety of people. Socrates practice of soul hygiene is similar. His soul is not dependent upon any doctrinal beliefs. This does not prevent him from having strong beliefs, as he shows in the *Meno*.

> I do not insist that my argument in right in all other respects,
> but I would contend at all costs both in word and deed as far
> as I could that we will be better men, braver and less idle, if
> we believe that one must search for the things one does not
> know, rather than if we believe that it is not possible to find
> out what we do not know and that we must not look for it.
> (86 b-c)

He is committed to the inquiry but not to any of its results, which always remain fallible. His self-image is an ongoing part of this inquiry. He follows the Delphic oracle's admonition to "Know Thyself", as he says in the *Phaedrus,* and realizes he has not yet accomplished this. He does not know whether he has a simple or complex nature; he is not rooted in any one image of it. He tries new and varied experiences, such as the Bendis religious festival, walking outside the city's walls or being gussied up with bath and sandals and attending a celebrity's dinner. He turns each of these into a self-conscious experience through discourse. And he trades ideas and criticisms with an endless variety of people, as the parade of dialogue partners shows. Socrates' soul hygiene is not only similar to psychological therapy but also to modern scientific method. Perhaps all three are just good thinking. One tries to limit the distortions caused by prejudice and habit by multiplying the types of conditions under which an experiment holds, and to engage in the experimental process as large a community as possible to clarify what exactly is being observed and what it means.

I would like to conclude this discussion of the death of the soul with a look at one of Plato's more outrageous Hades stories, that in the *Phaedrus* of the winged, disembodied souls flying about the heavens with the gods. It begins with another disquieting "proof" for the immortality of the soul. Many commentators accept this as again reflecting Plato's religious beliefs. "The immortality of the soul is established by an argument which Plato regarded as incontrovertible," and "from whatever source he may have derived his justification for believing in personal immortality, there can be no doubt that he did believe in it".[12] Yet the first commentator admits that the argument is poor. "Stripped of the terminology of the Ideal theory, this amounts to saying that the notion of life is bound up with the notion of soul, and what it really yields is not (as Socrates maintains) the conclusion that the soul is immortal but the tautological proposition that so long as soul exists it is alive".[13] This interpretation runs that Plato must have believed in the immortality of the soul because he offered proofs for it. But then the proofs are shown to be pitiful, and some excuse must be made for Plato's deficient thinking. Hackforth rationalizes that at least Plato's effort here is more empirical than his previous metaphysical proofs in the *Phaedo* and thus prepares the way for Aristotle's later Prime Mover argument for god's existence[14].

In the context of this dialogue, offering this proof makes good sense. Socrates' "proof" that the soul is immortal because it is ever-moving is just enough to get the attention and agreement of the exercise-conscious but lazy Phaedrus. He wants to be self-moving but finds himself continually being moved by others: the speech of Lysias, the order to exercise by Eryximachus, the seduction letters he attracts, Socrates' suggestion to talk rather than walk. The self-movement principle is weak in Phaedrus; he needs to strengthen his soul. Just as Socrates distanced himself from his "proof" by saying, "*If* it has been established that what moves itself is identical with soul" (246a), so he distances himself from claiming that the soul-life he is about to describe must be true. Only the gods, he says, could give an adequate description, so Socrates will have to settle for using an image, a self-conscious mixture of truth and fiction.

Socrates goes on to develop this image of the soul as a composite of a charioteer and two winged horses, one noble and the other base. The disembodied horses pull the charioteer around the heavens, traveling with a group of like souls under the leadership of one of the twelve Olympian gods, minus the goddess Hestia who, being a home-body, must of course stay home. When hungry, the gods fly to the top of the heavens and step out on the other side to be nourished by the metaphysical principles that there exist. Remember metaphysics means beyond or outside of nature, and it examines such questions as why is there something rather than nothing, which cannot be answered from within nature. These gods feed their traditional fare of nectar and ambrosia to their horses, while nourishing themselves on the rational principles of existence. Strange gods! Gods who demonstrate that philosophy is not only linked with the invisible world of the dead, but it also serves as the divine pastime of the gods.

The non-divine souls, distracted by their horses, struggle to see "the things that are," the realities beyond the heavens. The most godlike sees most, some see only some and most are too distracted to see any. When reincarnated the most godlike will be free from harm, protected by their vision of the truth. Those with partial vision are reincarnated according to how much they saw. Those who saw the most become lovers of wisdom, beauty or music, while those who saw the least become tyrants. At the end of their life all will be judged, punished or rewarded, and then reincarnated again. In the story one can progress up the scale of occupations at 1000-year intervals or, in our reality, within one's present life. It is a nine-level scale of increasing self-knowledge, from the pseudo-self of the tyrant lost in a sea of ever-shifting desires (Meno, Thrasymachus, Callicles), to the sophist so consumed by the probable that he has given up on the real, to the craftsman who, like a sophomore (wise fool), thinks that because he knows a little he knows everything, to the poet whose creative products are like the real but have no means to distinguish them from fantasies, to the religious mystic who sees there is more to the world than our knowledge of this moment, to the trainer or doctor of the body who understand the need for nutrition and care, to the man of affairs in the city pursuing his account (*logos*) of life, to the wise ruler who can articulate and defend the laws of his city, and finally to the lover of wisdom or beauty or a Muse-inspired lover, perhaps like Plato's brothers in the *Republic*. Those at this highest level can deal with ideas as they are in themselves, rather than through systems, such as defining justice through a system of law, or analogies, such as comparing the care of the soul to that of the body. Possibly these nine steps could also form another system, such as the stages of maturing from childhood to adult, but here they are career options determined by how we understand our relation to our social and natural environment. And as any one such understanding dies, we are reincarnated into another, either higher or lower.

This reincarnation is not in the service of the fear of god, as those who here interpret Plato as religious want us to believe, but rather in the service of our fear of ourselves. We hold ourselves prisoners to a way of life or belief because we are afraid that we either cannot change or will not be any better off if we do. We are not willing to risk, which philosophically means not willing to offer our ideas for criticism. We hide, dissemble, make plausible excuses, and begin to sound like rhetoricians. Reincarnation is the understanding that, as we have seen before in the *Phaedo* story of the tailor who wears out several cloaks during his life, our ideas wear out, no longer fit, cease being effective and need to be remade or replaced. (87b-88b) The *Phaedrus* story here continues on to the second incarnation, which is not dictated by the gods as the first one above but is a choice that the soul makes, much like that in the *Republic's* Myth of Er. After a life that was either unsatisfactory or uncertain of how its success was achieved, if the only thing that we know is failure or luck, how do we pick the next? Philosophy, the participation in a community of critical inquiry, is the answer both in the moment of death and in that of life. After discovering how the philosopher overcomes death, we are now prepared to examine how she pursues life.

II. Life

Now that we have seen that ideas can die, we are in a better position to examine how they live. As we explore this life of ideas, we will also discover more about what Plato thinks philosophy is and how one goes about doing it. In the dialogues ideas both have a life, that is, they are described as having behaviors similar to those of living bodies, and they also come to life, that is, they are incarnated. The character of Socrates is, at least in part, the idea of philosophy brought to life, and his activities demonstrate aspects of the life of an idea as well. Just as an athletes' body needs competition to test its worth, so does Socrates with his ideas. Ideas are always on the alert, to be tested, nourished, overthrown. The ideas in the *Symposium*, for example, behave in the ways that the bodies of the speakers, here neutralized by hangovers, usually do; they intoxicate, impregnate, nourish, seduce, put on special clothes, etc. The flute playing prostitutes are sent away and replaced by the rival speeches, which compete to seduce the minds of the audience.

Ideas are not passive objects in our minds, like documents in a safety deposit box. They have needs such as maintenance and efficacy and offer benefits such as guidance and security. Being alive, they interact with each other; they are dynamic. There is continual adjustment between new arrivals, old standbys, and the world of experience.

In the previous section we saw how Plato used a suggestive system of religious vocabulary and images to help discuss the philosophic experience of the periodic death and rebirth of our ideas and minds. Just as these images made use of the notion that ideas and souls have a body-like existence in the next world, so, when Socrates goes on to discuss the life of our ideas and minds in this world, he borrows the language used to describe the more familiar activities of our bodies. Ideas provide nourishment, like the feasts of words in the *Republic*, *Gorgias*, and *Symposium*. They require testing to show what they are worth, similar to an athletic competition and illustrated by the trial in the *Apology*, the horse race in the *Republic* and the matching of wits in the *Protagoras*. They enter into our lives with powerful emotions, as when we gaze in wonder at absolute beauty in the *Symposium* or we throb and sweat as we approach the incarnation of this beauty in the *Phaedrus*. They wrestle in the *Euthydemus*, intoxicate the guests at Agathon's *Symposium* and have sexual relations when speech impregnates another's mind, as in the *Theaetetus'*[15] midwife image and Agathon's seduction of Socrates' idea in the *Symposium* (175c).

Ideas are a general force in our lives, directing us for well or ill, as with Meno's ideas of power and the goods it acquires, Thrasymachus' or Callicles' idea of advantage, and Socrates' idea of the good presented in its several images in the *Republic*. The need to monitor this basic directing function and minister to its health brings us to one of the most pervasive images of the life of ideas, that of Socrates as a doctor of the soul, attending to the health of its ideas. Socrates' allegiance to Apollo, the god of medicine, emphasizes this special role. Apollo plays a significant role at several critical moments in Socrates' life. His oracle at Delphi sends Socrates on his life's mission to answer the riddle, "No one is wiser than Socrates." Diotima, who taught Socrates everything he knows about love, seems to be an Apollonian figure with her knowledge of the divine and concern with disease, as when she delayed the plague in Athens. [16] And finally the festival of Apollo extends Socrates' life for several weeks after his conviction.

Socrates' Apollonian medical mission is to convince others that ideas do play a significant role in our lives and that their health and nurture matters. "Submit yourself bravely to reason as you would to a physician," Socrates tells Polus in the *Gorgias* (475d). When the idea

46

of the city in the *Republic* becomes sick and fevered with Glaucon's demands for a more luxurious lifestyle, this illness is treated by purging the excess (399e). Phaedrus in his dialogue has started a new exercise program, realizing that he must be more careful about what he does with his aging body but still willing to take any idea into his mind without considering the consequences. In the *Republic* Socrates calls ideas drugs, especially a well-constructed and supported lie which the audience is unable to detect (382a-d). In the *Phaedo* ideas are magical, safeguarding charms, as Socrates calls the Pythagorean fairytales which he examines as proofs for the immortality of the soul (77e-78a). Hippocrates, Socrates' young friend in the *Protagoras*, carefully screens what food he eats but is careless about the nutritive value of the ideas he allows into his mind. He thinks he can be nourished on sophistry without becoming a sophist (313a-314c).

This soul doctor both ministers to the health of other people's ideas and exemplifies the state of healthiness in himself. A good way to follow Plato's presentation of the life of the mind is to observe Socrates' activities in the dialogues. The life of Socrates' character is in some way the life of the mind. To better understand this, we must re-examine the distinction between the historical and the dramatic Socrates.

The historical Socrates, who wrote nothing, presents an even more mysterious figure than Plato, who did write but in such an indirect and confusing manner. Of this Socrates we have three descriptions from people who directly knew him, each writing for different reasons and presenting different portraits. The comic playwright Aristophanes wrote a farce called "The Clouds" in 423 in which he lampoons sophists and nature philosophers. He presents Socrates as believing that the clouds are divinities and operating a sleazy school for profit with instruction in deceptive rhetoric and humbug scientific theories on such subjects as flea flatulence. Xenophon in his *Memorabilia*, *Apology* and *Symposium* presents the opposite extreme, a Socrates who is so prosaic and moralizing, so full of common sense and good will that he could never be a threat to anyone, much less the city as a whole.

The real Socrates probably exists between these two caricatures of the charlatan and the Unitarian minister. The third characterization, that by Plato, occupies a more middle space. He bothers people but does not charge them for it. How far this character is meant to be historical is currently a great controversy among commentators. The most popular approach is to determine which dialogues Plato wrote first and then claim that these early works present an accurate portrait, on the assumption that Plato is here mainly reporting the ideas and methods of his teacher. The assumption continues that as Plato's ideas mature and grow apart from those of Socrates, then the character Socrates separates from the historical one and either becomes Plato's direct mouthpiece or a representative of his evolving notion of philosophy.

This approach shares in the question begging to which we are continually driven by the lack of an accurate intellectual biography of either Socrates or Plato. We do not know the order in which the dialogues were written or the time intervals showing how long Plato had to mature between them.[17] Some dialogues mention historical events and therefore were written after they occurred, but how much after, no one knows. The common response is that someone either assumes a development in Plato and arranges the dialogues to illustrate this, or, contrariwise, they assume an order to the dialogues and then contrive a development in Plato to match this. Both ways have given important attention to interesting details in his writing and to the connections between the dialogues. But neither presents a compelling case.[18] Socrates' character can be both historical in inspiration and Platonic in function without these traits being divided chronologically and without being wholly defined by either. Plato could have a consistent idea about this character's role which could continue throughout the dialogues with their apparent swings in dramatic intensity and complexity, the apparent move away from aporetic (puzzling) endings to dialectical conclusions, and even the relative silence or absence of Socrates himself.

I would like to support the consistent character option. The character of Socrates, at least in part, represents the idea of philosophy itself come to life and working in the world. He is something other than simply human, just as the Homeric heroes Achilles and Odysseus were. He presents a single dimension of being human in such a way that we can see its essential role in our lives, but also how difficult it is to stay in this role, and even whether it is always desirable. Just as most of us would not want a slaughtering or deceiving Homeric hero living next door to us, so we would think twice about having to face Socrates everyday. Socrates is all philosophy all of the time. He places a demand upon us to keep realizing our philosophic nature, yet himself lives this nature in such an isolated and monomaniacal manner that our lives barely seem to touch his. He has been called "cold" in his aloofness from everyday human affairs and emotions and in his tunnel vision that finds only life's most critical issues worth discussing.[19]

Plato chooses this Socrates not to represent himself but to represent philosophy. He is the undistracted and undivided love of wisdom. Whether it is the tasty treat of Agathon's or Cephalus' feast, the sexual treat of Charmides' or Alcibiades' naked body or the domestic treat of returning home to his family after being away with the army (*Charmides* 153a) or after the all night party in the Symposium, Socrates seems impervious to them all in his pursuit of philosophy. His god-like behavior illustrates philosophy as one of the human activities in which we come as close as we are able to being divine. In our efforts to give our lives order and meaning, we become creators of our world,[20] as when Descartes mimics the six days of Biblical creation in creating his rational order for life in the *Meditations* or as the speeches in the *Symposium* reflect the seven competing world orders of their creators. As we can create, we also have to live with the consequences of our creating and must critique the performances of our ideas. Socrates can maintain himself in this create-critique nexus beyond human endurance. When in camp with the army, for instance, he once stood in the same spot considering a solution and its consequences for an entire day and night, an action he repeats on a lesser scale while waiting for the dinner and small talk to end at Agathon's party. (*Symposium* 22c-d and 174d-175c).

Philosophy as Plato presents it through Socrates is an activity of necessarily endless striving (*eros*) for humans. Our mental creations are never complete and never stay put, which is why Socrates spends so much time reminding people that they still have more work to do. Whoever thinks they are making progress or actually attaining wisdom is persuaded by the Fellini-like parade of characters through the dialogues that, as in any scientific experiment, there are many ways to be wrong, and whatever happens to be working at this moment may turn out to be wrong as well. Scientific "truth" is only as good as the next experiment; the guiding ideas in our lives are only as good as the next account and defense we can give of them.[21] Socrates is always ready to start over, to take nothing for granted, to test his ideas and himself everyday.

Living against the background of the Athenian tragic theater festivals, there is a strong suggestion of the tragic hero about Socrates. Oedipus after his life had been turned inside out still refused to subordinate his inquiring mind to the will of the gods. Although Socrates is an associate of tragic figures like Alcibiades and grotesque ones like Critias, he does not seem to experience physical tragedy similar to theirs but is faced with an overwhelming mental one. As David Roochnik has put it, there is a tragedy of *logos*, of reason itself, "because it cannot achieve a moral techne (art, skill, technique), a stable body of reliable knowledge able to tell us, in fixed terms readily teachable to others, how we ought to live".[22] Plato knows that normal human beings

49

will be overcome at least occasionally by the continual thwarting of this most basic desire for stability and happiness. Socrates, as the greater than human ideal of the Athenian citizen, can face tragedy directly and continuously and not be destroyed by it. It is to participate in this strength that Plato presents us with this character and also, perhaps, to remind us of our limitations.

For many of us, we first meet Socrates in the *Apology*, where for both historical and dramatic reasons he must defend his way of life. The historical Socrates actually did go on trial before a large number of his fellow citizens, was found guilty and sentenced to death. This trial of Socrates for his life provides Plato with a unique opportunity to describe his mentor in action facing death and thereby to differentiate philosophy from rhetoric. There is a heated controversy over how much Plato could deviate from Socrates' actual words in making his defense. Generally those who think that this dialogue was written within a few months or years of the event feel that it must be close to Socrates' own words. Those who think its composition was later admit more creativity on Plato's part. This controversy, like most regarding Plato's biography, is insoluble with the information we now possess.

What we do possess in this dialogue is the strong portrait of a person who does this odd thing called philosophy, and with the oddness not removed or glossed over. Socrates is not being made pretty here. He is possessed by a *daimon* or inner voice who tells him what not to do. He spends his days accosting his fellow citizens and quizzing them about their ideas. He claims this invasion of other people's privacy is a divine mission. He has a family with which he spends little time but mentions it when convenient. He suggests by his singular commitment to seeking wisdom that he is better than other people, whom he berates for paying attention to material goods more than to the health of their souls. On first meeting Socrates, we might find ourselves ready to join in the muttering by the jury against this man.

The crustiness of Socrates soon becomes a reflection of our own crustiness. Philosophy enters the dialogue through the distinction Socrates makes between the unconscious crust of opinions or stereotypes the jury has formed during their lifetimes and the fully conscious judgment they are supposed to render in their legal role today. The ideas of Socrates and philosophy have had a life in the minds of the jury for many years. They laughed at the charlatan named Socrates in Aristophanes' play and passionately discussed the value of those wandering rhetoric teachers, the sophists, who offer the youth of a city short cuts to political success and then leave after having stirred up their hopes and pocketed their money (*Meno* 91b-92d). Sophists, philosophers, fancy talkers, these all amounted to the same thing in the popular opinion. But on this day, the people are on jury duty, an occasion when they could use some help finding the truth, and one where philosophy has the stage to make its case for providing this help.

Popular opinion is alive in the audience and has to be challenged to prove its worth before any more critical faculties can even begin to work. As discussed previously, we prefer to calculate rather than think. We prefer to use our habitual ideas rather than to test them and develop new ones. At his trial Socrates discusses the need to test our ideas and ourselves, while the trial itself presents a clear example of this process made primary. To be on trial is a philosopher's dream, to have his entire city demanding an account of his ideas and criticizing them, to have people spend the day with nothing to do except examine ideas and the people who hold them, and to have the citizens meet to consider what exactly is the good of their city. The law courts provided such an opportunity for philosophy, and this is what Plato has Socrates do, use the occasion to do philosophy with his fellow citizens.

What is the life of ideas and the mind portrayed here? This initial discussion in the dialogue emphasizes that we are always in the midst of our ideas. We cannot clear our minds of all ideas and then think, nor can we judge accurately unless we take into account our previous ideas concerning both what we are judging and how to go about doing this judging. Thus the traditional charges against Socrates reflect the limits we, and the jury, put upon our own inquiry: certain ideas are off limits to examination, my ideas and arguments are rhetorically pure and I expect the same from others, there are some areas of infection by rhetoric in our society but they are easily recognized and restricted. We know commercials, lawyers, politicians, and sophists can tell lies, but we expect teachers, textbooks and friends not to do so. Our lives are too busy for total inquiry, so we exempt from examination both those foundational ideas which are too risky, painful, and time consuming to change, as well as our method of reasoning that supports these ideas.

What sets Socrates on this risky course of self-examination which most of us avoid? Apollo's oracle tells him that no person is wiser than he is. Most people agree that humans are able to know the world as it is experienced, and that no one is particularly better at this. This is another claim of common sense that Socrates proceeds to turn on its head. As Meletus says here (24e) and Anytus repeats in the *Meno*, all Athenian citizens are equally able to instruct the youth about proper behavior (92e). Socrates turns this commonplace into an examination of what it is we claim that we all know. With the exception of certain skills developed by the craftsmen, most of this knowledge turns out to be opinion. The claim that we all know certain things turns out to be that we all think that we know, and that the statement that "no one is wiser" refers not to an equality of knowledge but of ignorance. If we all knew what everyone else knows, then this shared knowledge would make inquiry ineffective and unnecessary. Our shared ignorance would seem to have the same result until we realize that inquiry can be effective in developing well-founded opinions that, when true, serve equally well to guide us in life (*Meno* 97a-99c). Common sense prefers, but cannot attain, stable and reliable knowledge. Only after this fails does it turn, reluctantly, to philosophy and the work of creating reliable opinions and the constant criticism of maintaining them.

The ambiguity of the oracle's pronouncement that "no one is wiser" sets up the type of turnabout in our ideas that Socrates frequently makes. There are many ancient stories of the oracle's testing of people through its ambiguities. King Croesus was told that a great kingdom would fall if his army crossed the boundary river with his neighbor. In his greed he concluded that the kingdom would be his neighbor's, while after the fact it was his own. Here Socrates wonders if the oracle means that he is wiser than everyone else, the wisest of all. This is the interpretation he first suggests and supports with his claim that he alone knows that he does not know. But he gives away this lonely advantage to help others also realize how little they really know. He pushes the comparative "wiser" up to the superlative "wisest" in order to settle back to the positive and shareable "wise" with a better understanding. The world of ideas is a great democracy. "No one is wiser" does not segregate the wisest but unites us all in the same common wisdom and inquiry. We know that we do not know and have to seek together to find out what we can know.

That philosophy is of necessity democratic is essential to Plato's thought. Although democracy values freedom primarily for the pursuit of individual desires, this is also the realm where criticism is most unrestrained and potentially honest. It is no accident that the *Republic* takes place in the Piraeus suburb of Athens that was the democratic stronghold. In the descriptions of the ideal government and its degenerate forms in Book VIII of the *Republic*, democracy is the only regime where thinking is permitted to take place. The others have each defined their good and have no place for this inquiry. The ideal aristocracy of the philosophers becomes refined to the point where calculation replaces inquiry. There are systems for education, career selection and eugenics. A human mistake in the calculation of this last area, in the nuptial number that controls reproduction, will cause the system to break down. Our irresistible and ultimately tragic hope (as we saw in

Roochnik above) that reason will find a stable foundation for our lives is once again dashed. Being able to practice surviving such a wreck seems to be one of the reasons Plato had for constructing such a well-founded edifice. Socrates does not seem too dismayed that this "ideal" construction falls apart. "A city so composed is hard to be moved. But, since for everything that has come into being there is decay, not even a composition such as this will remain for all time; it will be dissolved" (546a).

Once the best can no longer reproduce itself, it will cease to be present in the city and no longer serve as the measure of all things. In the absence of what is known to be the best, it will be replaced, in the city and the soul, by what the culture deems most worthy--by honor. A timocracy or rule by the honored will take over. As the coherence of the culture and its notion of honor become strained, a more concrete notion of good emerges, the goods. Oligarchy, the rule of the few with the goods, becomes the ruling force. Next the many people without goods claim that their desires are also of value and assume power for the people, the demos. Their power is defined by their freedom, especially from limiting actions and desires, which explains why thinking is permitted. The people compete, as in modern democracies, to have the greatest desires and the means to satisfy them. When one is able to succeed beyond all others and enlist them as his helpers to achieve even greater satisfaction, his desires become the social rule and norm. He becomes a tyrant. As the tyrant rules over others, so is he ruled in turn by his desires. Socrates in the *Gorgias* describes the futility of trying to satisfy all of one's desires with the image of continually pouring water into a leaky jar (493b). In case we are still attracted to this life, it is further described as a "pelican's life", eating and defecating at the same time (494b). Four of these political and soul states are controlled by external values: the experts' best, the culture's honor, the goods owned by the few, or the desires of one powerful person. Only in a democracy is the notion of value up for grabs. Only here can inquiry occur.

Finding a philosophic need for democracy in Plato's writings stands in sharp contrast to his reputation as an anti-democratic aristocrat. After World War II Plato shared the blame with Nietzsche for helping Hitler develop his totalitarian ideas,[23] and it is a commonplace of current textbooks that philosophers can only be kings if they are not democrats.[24] This opinion reflects the tradition of literal interpretation that, as we have seen, takes Socrates' statements in the dialogues as an end product, as Plato's dogmatic assertions of the truth. This assumed authoritarian approach by Plato encourages his interpreters to find hierarchical systems in his thinking, which makes him seem more authoritarian and then more hierarchical, and so on.

Realizing the democratic elements in the dialogues will help break this closed, mutually reinforcing cycle of interpretation. These elements support an alternative philosophic interpretation that Socrates' statements are part of a process and cannot be understood in isolation. This process is similar in all the dialogues yet expressed differently according to the varying circumstances and participants in each. The purpose of philosophy here is to bring our ideas to criticism, and this process seems to take an extended period of orientation and practice to overcome the reluctance shown by Socrates' partners. Socrates' own purpose is to accomplish the examination of his own life and ideas. Many images of Plato, such as that in Gilbert Ryle's *Plato's Progress* where he arranges king of the hill argument contests, encourage us to see him as more competitive than cooperative.[25] Yet what Socrates keeps asking of his partners is to join him in the inquiry. They need one another to see through each other's conscious and unconscious defenses and tricks. Criticism by the best person would of course be best and perhaps even sufficient, but Plato has taken us to this spot many times by now. We do not know who is best. There is not a human "best" which can give an adequate and consistent account of itself. So any proposed aristocracy (rule of the best), even that of the philosophers, cannot adequately explain and justify itself. Philosophy requires a criticism based on pluralism and democracy more than dogma.[26]

Socrates democratically talks to everyone he encounters, but not everyone talks to him. Most people are too busy making money or running their lives and rarely take much, if any, time to talk with him or trouble about anyone else. Most people most of the time and all of us some of the time choose not to think. It is rarely in our interest to disrupt what we are doing. Socrates talks to everyone to help others identify their golden, self-ruling nature, as the Myth of the Metals calls it. In the *Republic* Socrates proposes that the city they are constructing could use a story, a noble and useful lie (382c-e), about the types of metal present in each person which would identify that person's basic nature. The rulers have gold in them, the auxiliaries have silver and the farmers and craftsmen have iron and bronze (415a-d). This story seems to justify a natural aristocracy, that some people are born to rule and others to be ruled, but the story self-destructs. Instead of the metals explaining the type of person, the person has to be carefully examined to determine what sort of metal is present. Golden parents should produce golden children, but this is not always the case.

The analysis of social classes in the story further breaks down due to the parallel with the soul. The metals distinguish not only types of people, but also parts of the soul. Thus each soul contains all of the metals. We all have a golden, reasoning nature that is usually obscured by our iron, acquisitive part. The gold rarely expresses itself because we are too busy getting the goods, but the gold is democratically present in everyone. What looks like a support for hierarchic stability and privilege turns out to be another argument for inquiry, the need to determine the traits that constitute a good ruler and then to carefully examine each person to find out if they are present. We, the readers who are hunting for the good ruler and the just man throughout the many pages of this book, know that such a task is hardly as easy as determining the presence of gold. This evaporating explanation illustrates a general pattern in the dialogues where accounts initially appear dogmatic but when examined breakdown internally. This superficial inflexibility always gives way to the need for a more flexible and responsive discourse that can examine beneath this surface. The next chapter on Plato's method will explore this pattern further.

The lives of ideas create much of the drama in the dialogues, centering upon Socrates as an illustration of how to live this "life of reason".[27] In this section we have watched him bring reason to life and will finish here with several more examples of the life of ideas from the *Republic*.

These ideas come to life not to replace the things of this world but to prepare us for working with them. The idea of injustice comes to life in the unjust man who hides his injustice by using the Ring of Gyges, just as the unjust rhetorician hides behind his just sounding words. He is chased throughout the dialogue and finally brought to light in the chapter on the tyrant, where the consequences of founding one's life upon the idea of injustice are illuminated. Thrasymachus, like Callicles in the *Gorgias*, believes he can change one aspect of his beliefs and behavior without it affecting the rest of his life. Having an advantage over others must be an advantage to himself. He only sees the goods he will get from others and not the losses he will suffer. The portrait of the tyrant in Book IX vividly depicts this life and losses. He is isolated in his own power and desires. He is only told what people think he wants to hear. His culture represents the extreme of systematized deception, just as that of philosophy represents one of truth telling. The need to secure the cooperation of our partners in inquiry demands that we be truthful to them in hopes that they will be truthful in return. There is no guarantee that truth will be told other than the bond of friendship and good will between those relying on each other's judgement. When

Meno asks Socrates what sort of answer he would give to a particular
question, he responds

> A true one, surely, and if my questioner was one of those
> clever and disputatious (eristic, competitive) debaters, I would
> say to him: "I have given my answer; if it is wrong, it is your
> job to refute it." Then, if they are friends as you and I are, and
> want to discuss with each other, they must answer in a manner
> more gentle and proper to discussion. By this I mean that the
> answers must not only be true, but in terms admittedly known
> to the listener. (75 c-d)

One goal of philosophy is to be able to communicate clearly so
that one can receive in return a worthwhile judgment on the ideas presented. While Callicles claims rhetorical flourishes will leave Socrates
dizzy and helpless, Socrates counters that it is truly spoken judgments
(here spoken by the gods) which will dazzle and cripple Callicles
(*Gorgias* 526e-527a). When confronted with a divine truth teller revealing the truth about his soul, he will not know how to respond because he is only used to the games of rhetoric. He is unaware that the
ideas one holds are not only moves on a gameboard but also have consequences in one's life. One of the main reasons for Socrates telling
most of the afterlife stories is to illustrate this notion of consequences.

The promised feast in Cephalus' house never arrives except in the
ideas they are consuming, a meal Socrates has consumed too quickly to
adequately digest in Book I, so Plato writes another nine books to
spread out the banquet (354b). The proposed torchlight relay race on
horseback similarly only occurs as Plato's brothers pass back and forth
the light of inquiry they are using to hunt for justice. The idea of the
city is born and nurtured, becomes fevered and is purged, reaches ma-
turity only to find waves of criticism, realizes in mid-life that criticism
is actually beneficial and needs to be built in to its life and thus makes
the apolitical philosophers the rulers. Just as most citizens are too busy
making money to care about their souls, so philosophers are too busy
caring for their souls to be concerned with politics. They do it only to
further their interests in social stability, a large educated class (The
more philosophers, the less time each has to spend ruling the city.), and
open communication. They do it so as not to be limited by the rule of a
worse person, which is the same reason we seek to test our ideas, so
that we are not ruled by a worse one when a better one is possible.

III. Rhetoric – Part 2

Although Socrates claims that there is an "an old quarrel between philosophy and poetry" motivating the last book of the *Republic*, the most common quarrel we find in the dialogues is between philosophy and rhetoric. Socrates speaks with major sophists in four dialogues and with minor ones in several more, usually trying to clarify what rhetoric is and how it differs from philosophy. Other dialogues such as the *Phaedrus* and the *Symposium* contain extensive rhetorical displays and commentary. Now that the ideas and arguments of philosophy have come to life, in order to truly have their own life, they need to show how they are any different from the self-serving arguments of rhetoric.

In the minds of many Athenians philosophers were sharp talkers and logic choppers just like the sophists, and they thought there was no real difference between them. Socrates in the *Apology* is accused of being a sophist who makes the weaker argument appear the stronger. Aristophanes in his play *The Clouds* uses Socrates as his model of a sophist who encourages his students to employ such creative reasoning as "the way to avoid having to pay my debts is to hire a witch to capture the moon, and then since the end of the month (the moon's cycle) will never arrive, I will not have to pay what is due on the first of the month".[28] When Socrates arrives at the home where the sophists are staying in the *Protagoras*, he is taken for a sophist by the doorkeeper. In the *Phaedrus* the distinction between philosophy and rhetoric is an explicit theme, while the competitive love speeches of the *Symposium* examine this more implicitly. The *Sophist* pursues a lengthy, humorous and confusing classification of human beings and their activities, arriving at an uneasy distinction between the deceiving sophist and the truth seeking philosopher and statesman. We now need to investigate this distinction further, especially why philosophers must be committed to seeking the truth, just as we have examined previously its commitments to criticism in the death of ideas and to democracy in the life of ideas.

As philosophy comes to life in its practicing being dead, it has a difficult time when alive in distinguishing itself from its near relative rhetoric or sophistry. While the sophists, like Evenus in the *Phaedo*, clearly have no interest in engaging in the practice of death, their other interests do seem to parallel those of philosophy (61b-c). They flourish in a democracy where new ideas can be discussed in public. They attract the youth of the city, particularly those with political expectations. They raise questions about the foundations of traditional values and spread cultural relativism. Their practice requires a certain facility with language and logic. Although their presentations may be clear, they leave a degree of confusion in their wake. One interest is clearly different, that rhetoric succeeds by manipulating a given system of values, measuring anything from beauty to truth, while philosophy, at least in Socrates, seems to keep trying to construct in mutuality such systems. Our effort to distinguish these two may end not so much by separating them as by one absorbing the other.

Rhetoric and philosophy look and sound very similar, if not the same. Socrates uses rhetorical devices, taking advantage of the unexpected meanings and connections he squeezes out of language and forcing his partners to agree with the logic of his statements even while they question the applicability of his conclusions to real life. Hippias' complaint is typical "Oh, Socrates! You're always weaving arguments of this kind. You pick out whatever is the most difficult part of the argument, and fasten on to it in minute detail, and don't dispute about the whole subject under discussion" (*Hippias Minor* 369c).

We can see how similar they are in practice by comparing some examples. In the *Symposium* Agathon makes use of his sophistic training to fix on an ambiguity in the argument and twist it his way. He gives two good examples in his speech. This is how he proves that Love is self-controlled.

> Everyone admits that self-control is mastery over pleasures and desires, and that no pleasure is stronger than Love. If then all pleasures are weaker than Love, Love must be the master and they his subjects. So Love, being master over pleasures and desires, will be in a pre-eminent degree self-controlled. (196c)

The ambiguous phrase is "no pleasure is stronger than Love." As the argument runs past, the audience accepts this as "Love is the strongest of all pleasures," but then Agathon springs his conclusion by reversing it to mean "Love (not being a pleasure) is stronger than (all) pleasures." Since this is a possible meaning of the phrase, we are convinced by the form but left uneasy by the content. In his second example, he is proving the courage of Love.

> As for courage, Love "more than matches Ares," the god of war. It is not Ares who captured Love, but Love who captured Ares, lover of Aphrodite to wit, according to tradition. Now the capturer is superior to the captive, and the capturer of the

bravest of all other beings will necessarily be the bravest of all beings whatsoever. (196d)

Here the ambiguity turns on the phrase "the capturer is superior to the captive." The capturer is superior in this one situation having defeated the captive in one area of competition: wits, tricks, strength, patience or here sexuality. Because the capturer is superior in one area does not mean she is superior in any other area, much less all other areas, yet this is where Agathon goes. Since the capturer is superior, she must be braver as well as superior in any other quality you could mention. Again the meaning Agathon wants is in his phrase, so we accept it and, although uneasy, we cannot dwell on such vague doubts while we are trying to keep up with the rest of the argument.

Socrates, following the geometry demonstration with the slaveboy in the *Meno*, similarly proposes a hypothesis to help them examine whether virtue can be taught. The problem turns on the relation between what is teachable and knowledge, and Socrates says, "Or is it not plain to anyone that men cannot be taught anything but knowledge?" Socrates can cajole and bully his audience as well as the sophists. When he says something is "plain" or "obvious" or "clear," we should be on alert, just as with Agathon's "everyone admits" above. Such phrases use our intelligence against itself, for if we do not see what is claimed to be clear, then we are made to feel that it is our fault.[29] Here the "anything but" phrase provides Socrates with enough ambiguity. Socrates is trying to complete a syllogism that ends with the premise "Virtue is knowledge" and the conclusion "Virtue is teachable." His major premise, then, should be "All knowledge is teachable," but the phrase he actually says is "All teachables are knowledge." If "all V is K" and "all T is K", then no conclusion follows. Socrates even calls attention to this hasty reasoning, but Meno is oblivious (88c). Later, however, he does begin to feel something is amiss and wonders "whether we have investigated this correctly" (96d).

Hippias' concerns and Meno's wonderings point up a significant difference under the similarity of these arguments. Socrates' arguments are questioned by his audience. He not only seems to welcome this but even specifically sets it up. Agathon's speech, however, seeks an emotional response more than an intellectual one from the audience; they should be carried away by the beauty of his words, just as by that of his person. That Socrates questions only Agathon after his speech highlights a change in the use of rhetoric here. For Socrates rhetoric *leads to* questioning instead of avoiding it. As it becomes an instrument of self-examination, it provides a clue to sort out these two experiences.

Sophists prefer giving longer speeches before large audiences with little opportunity for reflection or questions. This is Thrasymachus' strategy in his first long speech in the *Republic*. Having spoken "he had it in mind to go away, just like a bathman, after having poured a great shower of speech into our ears all at once" (344d). Plato's sophists say they need long speeches to fully express their ideas and are always ready to give one, while they reluctantly participate in Socratic question and answer. The sophist wants his own person to be as little noticed as possible, just as he makes his audience feel homogeneous and not individually responsible. His arguments should be transparent in the light of common sense and popular opinion and not attract attention to themselves. He needs to know and use the predispositions and prejudices of his audience. Indeed, the best argument is one that appears as though it is not even arguing; it just provides information or tells the facts. Rhetoric's first goal is to hide that it even is rhetoric.

Socrates, on the other hand, always prefers to speak one-on-one in relatively short statements and gain his partner's assent to each step of the argument. Socrates uses his conversations to intensify the focus on himself and his partners, to test people and the ideas that support them. "My object is to test the validity of the argument, and yet the result may be that I who ask and you who answer will both be tested" (*Protagoras* 333c). He disturbs his audience by calling their prejudices into question. Anytus in the *Meno* claims to know all about sophists without ever having met one, just like Meno thought he knew all about virtue and the slaveboy thought he knew how to do geometry. Anytus is opposed to the sophists because they undermine traditional values, but he does not understand that these values are the playthings of such clever speakers only because they had already become hollow. The sophists are the symptom, not the problem. In a similar way rhetoric is the symptom. It reveals the patches where we are over-reaching, where we have connected our ideas without proper evidence. It is like a litmus test for ignorance; its presence shows the absence of knowledge. Rhetoric when used by itself is self-concealing but when guided by philosophy can reveal both itself and the state of the soul it represents.

This interpretation helps explain why Socrates' rhetorical gamesmanship seems to rise highest in his several encounters with the famous sophists: Gorgias, Protagoras, Hippias and the lighterweights Thrasymachus and Euthydemus and his brother. These partners accuse him of using a common ploy of the sophists, to be impressive by defending a view clearly contrary to public opinion, common sense or logic.[30] In the *Gorgias* he argues that it is better to suffer wrong than to do it. In the *Hippias Minor* he says those who commit injustice voluntarily are better than those who do it involuntarily (376d). In the *Protagoras* he twists the famous poet Simonides' words to support his claim that no one does evil voluntarily. In the *Republic* he says that the advantage of the stronger is to care for those who are weaker. The sophist would take such unpopular positions so that he could show off his persuasive skills by convincing the crowd. Socrates takes his unpopular positions also to focus on his skills, but for their weakness rather than their strength, for their criticism. He wants to draw attention to how he is reasoning so that it will be questioned. In these contests of arguments, to expose a fault in Socrates' reasoning is to do him a favor. He makes people be on the look out for rhetoric instead of hiding it.

Socrates supports these unpopular views not just for display but also to be taken seriously. He proposes them rhetorically, so that his audience will be on their guard. When we know we are receiving rhetoric, we go into thinking mode. We become hunters of logic and illogic, one of Socrates' common images for his activity. This causes us to think about issues that previously were too well defended by our commitments in life to risk being upset. As we watch someone failing against Socrates' skill, we consider the possibility of our own failing. We are brought to consider risking an important idea in our life because we are faced with images of the greater risk we run if we do not. We do not want our beliefs ultimately supported by tricks, whether by those of Socrates or the sophists.

The revealing of rhetoric can lead not only to its own examination but to that of the life-supporting ideas that it is hiding and protecting as well. Thus Socrates is able to turn even rhetoric to his primary task, examining his life. In the *Phaedrus* Socrates explains how thorough this approach must be, as a true rhetoric requires knowledge of all types of people, all types of speech and how to properly match them.

> When (the rhetorician) is not only qualified to say what type of man is influenced by what type of speech, but is able also to single out a particular individual and make clear to himself that there he has actually before him a specific example of a type of character which he has heard described, and that this is what he must say and this is how he must say it if he wants to influence his hearer in a particular way--when, I say, he has grasped all this, and knows besides when to speak and when to refrain, and can distinguish when to employ and when to eschew the various rhetorical devices of conciseness and pathos and exaggeration and so on that he has learnt, then

and not till then can he be said to have perfectly mastered his art. (271e-272a)

If someone were to know all of this, he would have tremendous power, and the control of this power is the last aspect of rhetoric that we must examine. What assurance can there be that this power will be used for the good of the one who has it and for the society as a whole? Why should a society work to develop the abilities in its citizens if there is no control over whether these powers will be used for or against it? In the traditional notions of political power, aristocrats were born with the ability to govern and a commitment to the public good, reinforced by the culture in its epics, tragedies and religious ceremonies. In a timocracy (rule of the honorable) the notions of honor and shame so permeated the society that able people would be held in line by public praise and blame. For the oligarchy wealth reflected merit and carried with it the responsibility to use the wealth for social good. All of these forms of governing relied on some sort of involuntary control (blood, shame, duty) to limit the exercise of power, but as Socrates shows in *Republic* Book VIII these limits are unstable and subject to failure. Only democracy has a voluntary reason for limiting one's individual power, that by sharing power one gains the social stability that permits the fewest limitations to be placed upon the pursuit of individual desire. This stability, however, can be upset by individuals uniting into a faction or gang, concentrating their power in order to give them an advantage over others and better satisfy their own desires. If this faction gains power, it finds that the same logic applies to itself, with a competition among its own internal parts, until the strongest competitor emerges successful. Thus the tyrant comes into being, a man with no need and only limited ability to control his desires.

This problem about the way to control power for the benefit of the individual and society is a constant tension in Athenian society and in the dialogues. The story of Gyges in Book II of the *Republic* tells of a ring that turns a person invisible and the effect this has on him; he immediately embarks on a life of crime without fear of punishment. This is what rhetoric seems to enable its users to accomplish. As Adeimantus here points out in his description of the unjust man, the person who persuades others of his justice can practice injustice with impunity so long as he continues to plausibly define his actions as just.

To help resolve this, the time has arrived to discuss "The Cave," the most famous of Plato's images for modern readers and the one most repeated in textbooks and anthologies. Thus it is also the one most taken out of context and left to explain itself without its relations. First let's see the story and then examine the relations. In the beginning of Book VII of the *Republic*, Socrates "makes an image of our nature in its education and want of education" (514a). He describes human beings dwelling as prisoners in a cave. They are forced to look only forward. Behind them is a fire which provides light and a wall over which all the items we see in our world appear. Other people are carrying these objects and making noises appropriate to them. As they pass in front of the fire, they make shadows that are seen by the prisoners on the side of the cave in front of them. The prisoners experience these shadows and echoing sounds to be life.

It is then examined what would happen to a prisoner if he were freed. When he turned around and went to the cave opening, he would find moving his body painful, as he had previously been restrained, and be blinded by the sun's light on his darkness-adjusted eyes. In the dazzled state he could not clearly see or describe the things passing on the wall and would prefer to go back to the familiarity of the shadows. If such a freed prisoner were forced out of the cave and into the sun, he would gradually get accustomed to the greater light. He would again be able to see the shadows but now could also clearly see the things that made them, as well as the sources of light, the stars and the sun.

Socrates explains this ascent, with the usual disclaimer that "a god, perhaps, knows if it happens to be true," as "in the knowable the last thing to be seen, and that with considerable effort, is the idea of the good; but once seen, it must be concluded that this is the cause of all that is right and fair in everything... and that the man who is going to act prudently in private or in public must see it" (517b-c). The appearance of the idea of the good is the climax of the search for justice and the key to the solution of why be just or tell the truth. This idea appears when one is able to leave the cave and see things in a better light; it is the explanation that makes sense of all the rest.

Having an idea of the good is a fact of our psychological experience. Each of our lives is organized by a hierarchy of ideas that we use to make decisions. The most basic idea we have concerning our own welfare is our idea of our good. The most basic idea of the welfare of the universe (why things are the way they are) is our idea of universal good. This idea of our own good is the most critical idea for how we lead our lives. All of our actions follow from this idea, which is why Socrates makes the claim that we do not choose to do evil (*Protagoras* 345e), rather in such cases we only have a deficient idea of our own good. Because so many other ideas rest upon it, this idea of the good is buried deep inside our thinking and rarely considered, much less examined. It is the most critical idea for the "practice of dying and being dead" but also the most difficult to approach.

This middle section of the *Republic* gives us a series of images about this idea or at least its offspring (506e), the Sun, the Divided Line and the Cave. These occur at the critical point in the dialogue where the specially trained members of the ruling class are transformed from powerful rulers who could compel others to do their wishes into philosophers who have to be compelled even to use, much less abuse, their rule in the city. This transformation is the answer to the problem of injustice hiding as justice and other rhetorical concealing. This series of images illustrate in order our realizing that we have an idea of the good, that it is hidden under layers of images, beliefs, and calculations as the Line suggests, and that any move to examine this idea requires a removal from our regular life experiences out of the Cave.

The Cave experience is present in many dialogues, and we can see the beginnings of this transformation in such moments as when Meno begins to wonder in his dialogue (96d and 97c), or even better when Alcibiades in the *Symposium* describes the "snake bite" he received from Socrates (217e-218a). Socrates makes him examine his idea of the good by crushing his old one. Alcibiades thought he had the best mind in the best body and that anyone would want to take advantage of either. But when he offers himself to Socrates, he is turned down. The idea that organized his life is shredded. He is pushed to the verge of examining his life but falls back.

One of the most interesting places to observe the Cave and its consequences is the series of dialogues involving the sophists. Socrates flushes them out of their hiding by threatening their ideas of the good. We feel free to lie when manipulating other people's ideas, but want the truth when our own are at stake. Protagoras in his dialogue wants the virtues to be separable rather than basically the same so he can teach any one without including the others. Socrates argues that all virtues are essentially connected and makes Protagoras agree until only courage remains to be included. Courage is the virtue most important for rhetorical success; confidence is persuasive. As Socrates has become more rhetorical, especially his manipulating of the poem he interprets, Protagoras becomes less so. He even turns away from public opinion as his guide and examines his own idea (353a). At the end of the dialogue his idea has failed. He is at the door of the Cave and blinded by the light he would need to find a new idea. He has experienced the same "snake bite" as Alcibiades, and like him seems unable to completely pass through the door. When he realized that his own truth was at stake, he became a truth-seeker, if only for a moment.

There is an ending to the Cave story. If the person now used to the sun's light were to go back down into the cave, the dark would bother his sight as much as the light had before, and he would again be confused. If cave dwellers were to ask him what he had seen above, they would have no comparable experience that he could use to explain his own. They would say he came back confused and incoherent and would want nothing to do with his out-of-cave adventure. It is from these adventurers that the ranks of philosophers are filled. Their quest is to find the best light or *logos*, the one which illuminates the most. Ruling the city is a necessary pastime on the way to implementing the next breakout from our cave.

Notes

1. T. S. Kuhn, *The Essential Tension* (Chicago: Chicago University Press, 1977) p. xii.
2.   There is an important point which nearly all the histories of philosophy persistently overlook. The attentive reader who looks below the surface will find that Plato usually limits his dogmatic affirmation to one or two elementary principles of logic or morals. He concludes nearly all his subtlest speculations, his myths, and his symbolisms with some such formula as this;"The rest I would not positively affirm; of this only I am sure." And that of which he is sure proves to be only some indispensable presupposition of elementary logic or ethics.
Paul Shorey, *Platonism Ancient and Modern* (Berkeley: University of California Press, 1938) 12.
3. This is one of Socrates' arguments for the immortality of the soul in the *Phaedo*. It is a good ad hominem argument for anyone who speaks Greek. To us it sounds like a simplistic play on words, but reveals an aspect of the *psuche's* nature, that it cannot co-exist with death.
4. Aristotle, *Metaphysics*, 987a1
5. Martha Nussbaum examines this theme of the fragility of happiness in the philosophies of Plato and Aristotle in her book *The Fragility of Goodness: Luck and Ethics in Greek Tragedy and Philosophy* (Cambridge: Cambridge University Press, 1986).
6. *Apology* 29e, 38a, 39d and *Protagoras* 333c
7. G. Mylonas, *Eleusis and the Eleusinian Mysteries* (Princeton: Princeton University Press, 1961) 245.
8. R. W. Sharples, *Plato: Meno* (Chicago: Bolchazy-Carducci Publishers, 1985) 145-149.

9. Socrates' speaking partners often respond with a long series of short innocuous assents to his statements. Some critics, notably Cornford, feel this is such poor drama and philosophy that they edit it out it as unnecessary. These repeated assents reflect the mind set of the partner in the dialogue which is often shared by the reader as well. We often "yes-yes-yes" as we read along which is part of Plato's strategy. We cruise along in habit mode until we are shaken out of our slumbers.

10. Death is welcomed but not suicide. We are too involved with our ideas to properly judge their worth, particularly when under mental strain. Thus we should not kill our own ideas but let them be tested in conversation between friends.

11. For the power of this idea of speech and reasoning, compare the beginning of the Book of John in the *Bible*, "In the beginning was the *logos* and the *logos* was with God and the *logos* was God." Revised Standard Version (New York: Nelson, 1933)

12. Hackforth, *Phaedrus*, (Cambridge: Cambridge University Press, 1972) 64 and R. K. Gaye, *The Platonic Conception of Immortality*, 39, as quoted in Hackforth.

13. Hackforth, op. cit., p. 68.

14. Many commentators use Aristotle to orient their work on Plato, working backward from Aristotle's comments on Plato and then forward again toward Aristotle as the fruition of what is best in Plato. In whatever Aristotle wrote, he was always explaining his own philosophy, and whatever comments he made, he made for his own reasons and not necessarily to offer us an objective view of his teacher. We tend to polarize the ideal-seeking Plato vs. the empirical Aristotle, creating caricatures unfair to both. They did have different interests but not necessarily the different visions of philosophy or the world frequently attributed to them. Shorey summarizes this nicely.

> (Coleridge's) aphorism that every man is born either a
> Platonist or an Aristotelian is broadly true, yet not for the
> reasons usually alleged in its support. It is not true that Plato
> is a dreamer and Aristotle a student of fact and reality. It is
> not true that Aristotle is a reasoner and Plato a mystic and
> enthusiast. It is true that Plato is a reasoner, an artist, a poet, a
> mathematician, and a symbolist, while Aristotle is a logician,
> a biologist, a classifier, and an encyclopedist.

Paul Shorey, op. cit., 8.

For a good discussion of the spell that Aristotle has held over many commentators, see Drew Hyland, *Finitude and Transcendence in the Platonic Dialogues* (Albany: SUNY Press, 1995) 169-170.

15. Cf. the New Testament story of the impregnation of Mary by the Word of God.

16. An interesting possibility is that here too we jump to Plato's bait too quickly. The most famous plague, of course, was that which ravaged Athens at the beginning of the Peloponnesian War in 430. But could Diotima be defending against another type of plague, perhaps that of rhetoric which infects language with deception? Then her seemingly divine means of maintaining the health of the city are a forerunner of philosophy. Her initiation or indoctrination of Socrates into the truth about love is full of domineering pronouncements which she keeps pushing Socrates to challenge (206e, 207c, 208c), much as he does later to his own audiences, and Plato does to us.

17. Dating the Platonic dialogues has been a cottage industry for over a century. The best approach here as elsewhere is to find out the dimensions of the debate and the relative evidence on all sides. Two good places to begin are Jacob Howland, "Re-reading Plato: The Problem of Platonic Chronology," *Phoenix* 45, no.3 (1991): 189-214 and Leonard Brandwood, "Stylometry and Chronology" in R. Kraut, ed., *The Cambridge Companion to Plato* (New York, 1992): 90-120.

18. This question has supported many scholars and produced many books recently, and I do not mean to minimize the issues here. Since there are so many fine discussions, the interested reader should consult a comprehensive bibliography like that in H. Benson (ed.), *Essays on the Philosophy of Socrates* (New York, 1992).

19. Gregory Vlastos, *Socrates, Ironist and Moral Philosopher*, (Ithaca: Cornell University Press, 1991), and Martha Nussbaum's review in *The New Republic*, September 16 & 23, 1991, pp. 34-40.

20. It must be remembered that the Greek gods did not create the stuff of the world but only arranged the stuff that has always been here. The Judeo-Christian idea of a god who creates the universe out of nothing would have been considered absurd.

21. True belief is just as good as knowledge in directing our lives except that it is less likely to remain stable. The accounts by which we support our beliefs are subject to change and could even abandon us, like the statues of Daedelus described in the *Meno* (97d-98a).

22. David Roochnik, *Of Art and Wisdom* (University Park, Pa.: Penn State Press, 1996), xii. This quote refers to his first book *The Tragedy of Reason* (New York, 1990). Both books promote the Platonic vision of philosophy as challenging our fundamental ideas.

23. The most famous example of this accusation is Karl Popper's *The Open Society and Its Enemies* (Princeton: Princeton U. Press, 1966).

24.   Plato's fundamental vision is hierarchical and aristocratic, rather than egalitarian and democratic. His epistemology and metaphysics reflect and encourage this kind of highly discriminating orientation... If you believe in the fundamental equality of all people, you may be suspicious of Plato's belief in the superiority of those who have supposedly escaped the Cave and seen the Good. If you are skeptical about the possibility of any human being discovering the "truth," you will probably have difficulty with the idea that only these exceptional, enlightened individuals are more fit to govern than the rest of us.

Douglas Soccio, *Archetypes of Wisdom*, 3rd ed. (Belmont, Ca.: Wadsworth, 1998) 138-9. And if you have these reactions, it may be because Plato is awakening your critical abilities.

25. Gilbert Ryle, *Plato's Progress* (Cambridge: Cambridge University Press. 1966)

26. Three decades ago the American Philosophical Association went through a long similar discussion whether this profession can afford domination even by a majority, much less an aristocracy, without losing the critical edge which only the widest participation provides. The Association finally decided for more inclusion, and this is the pattern we repeatedly find in the dialogues.

27. This reflects the title of John Herman Randall's helpful introduction *Plato: Dramatist of the Life of Reason* (New York: Columbia, 1970)

28. Aristophanes, *The Clouds*, tr. Arrowsmith (New York: Mentor, 1962) 70.

29. We easily fall into this way of marshaling extra-logical support for our arguments. When the editor of the Hackett edition introduces the translation of the *Apology*, he uses "obvious," "surely" and "certainly" in the space of three sentences to support his argument for the historical accuracy of this dialogue. When such words creep into our arguments, it may well be a symptom that we are exceeding our evidence.

30. Gorgias was known for presenting a speech praising Helen as being innocent of any wrong and not responsible for starting the Trojan War.

Three
The Medium of the Dialogue

> Men grow weary of the very perfection of Plato, the polished
> surface of the unfailing literary art, the mastery of the
> inevitable dialectic, the sense of intellectual adequacy or
> superiority, the perfect reasonableness, the entire absence of
> pseudo science and a technical and system-building
> terminology for the mind to play with, the ironical evasion of
> unprofitable discussion of ultimates in symbolism and myth.
> And so they find a certain pleasure in the Stoic pedantry and
> commonplace.
>
> - Paul Shorey [1]

    Plato wrote his philosophy in the form of dialogues, some 29 or
so in number, with several more possibly by him and a dozen or so
forgeries in his style.[2] He may have also written a few letters explaining his political activities in Syracuse and given a few public presentations, the most famous being a "Lecture on the Good," which
apparently few people understood. But his legacy that we have to work
with is the dialogues. He could have written in the poetry or aphorisms
of his predecessors or the systematic treatise style of his pupil Aristotle,
but he chose to tell stories about conversations. Now that we have seen
philosophy at work in the dialogues and its role in the death and life of

our ideas, we can examine why a philosopher might choose this form of writing and how it succeeds.

I. Literary Background

This section will discuss the sources for the dialogue style that Plato developed. In Plato's intellectual environment there were several literary forms which are incorporated into the style of his dialogues. Understanding the elements of epic poetry, tragedy, comedy, history and memoirs which Plato blended into his form will help us to understand better the contribution of each.

Among the stories in the often-imaginative biographies of Plato is one that he wrote tragic dramas before turning to philosophy. There is a similar story for Aristotle that he wrote dialogues before realizing that he should be writing treatises. In Aristotle's case we have fragments of his dialogues, while we have no record of Plato's tragic plays. Some commentators feel that the *Phaedo* is his dialogue most like a tragedy and the *Symposium* most like a comedy. The *Symposium* concludes with a discussion whether the same author could write in both of these forms and reflects Plato's involvement with these genres. That he could represent the characters and compositions of the comedian Aristophanes and the tragedian Agathon so well in the *Symposium* demonstrates his own abilities as a playwright and may suggest that he is revealing some autobiography here.[3] Whether he ever did write plays or not, it is clear that he wrote in the context of the great Athenian tragic festivals. All of Athens could attend these civic and religious performances, with over 30,000 attending Agathon's play two days before the action in the *Symposium*. Plato's audience was familiar with both the drama of the theater and the dramatic recitals of Homer's epic poems. They were used to hearing multi-layered stories that both entertained and addressed moral, political and religious issues.

Increasingly the tragedies and comedies included extended rhetorical exchanges, from the "new logic" learned by Strepsiades' son in the *Clouds* to the argument between Medea and Jason over who did the greater service to the other in Euripides' *Medea*. The debates described in the historical recreations of Herodotus and Thucydides, like Plato, use actual historical figures saying the sorts of things that they actually did say. Including such probabilities in history was common and different from the stories of Homer's ancient culture heroes, which many Athenians considered to be fictional. The tragedies reworked much of this epic material. The comedies used caricatures of living people, with just enough historical accuracy here so that they would be recognized. This bawdy humor mixed slap stick with sophistication, flatulence and defecation with discussions of waging peace or the soul's immortality. Any source of humor was fair game, making fun of people's names, relatives, physical qualities, occupations, reputation, sexuality, etc.; the more ludicrous, the better. Reading Aristophanes' comedies is an essential preparation for reading Plato, just as Plato was informed by these comedies and their raucous style before he wrote his own works.

All of these elements are mixed into Plato's style. He tells stories about historical characters, combining history and fiction. He tells them against the background of the epics, frequently playing with Homer's stories, as when Socrates enters the house of the sophists in the *Protagoras* and describes the scene using the language of Odysseus visiting Hades in the *Odyssey* (315b-d). When Socrates picks up Aristodemus on his way to Agathon's party in the *Symposium*, he describes them as heroic fighters on their way to Agamemnon's house (174b-c). When Simmias and Cebes attack Socrates' argument in the *Phaedo*, he compares himself and Phaedo to Heracles enlisting Iolaus to help him fight two battles at once (89c). Sometimes the allusion is less explicit, as in the opening of the *Phaedo* when the story of Theseus saving twelve youths from being sacrificed to the Minotaur in the labyrinth is retold. Here the dozen or so youths that are visiting Socrates in prison also need to be saved from a similar half-rational monster, the bogeyman of death. Plato moves the world of Homer's epics from the clash of spears and bodies to that of words and ideas.

This new realm of heroic competition is a little less grim than the gore of the hundred suitors slain by Odysseus to purify his home in the *Odyssey* or the river Skamandros complaining because Achilles clogged it with dead bodies in the *Iliad*. There is room for humor. When Eryximachus (literally, the warrior against eructations, belches and hiccups) is among the combatants in the *Symposium*, his name is too inviting a target to be ignored, and Plato sets him in battle against Aristophanes' hiccups. Plato frequently plays upon the names of his characters. Meno (to remain) will not remain and be initiated into the Mysteries of philosophy. Meletus (care) does not care for the youths that he says in the *Apology* he is trying to save from Socrates. Cephalus (head) is not sure how to carry out the duties as head of his family in the *Republic*. Theaetetus (spectator) in his dialogue presents the notion that knowledge is perception. Thrasymachus is a "wild fighter" in the *Republic*, and Polus is an undisciplined "colt" in the *Gorgias*. Any good edition of a dialogue should explain the English meanings of the

Greek names, thus preparing us for at least some good puns, if not entire turns of the plot.

There are also others types of humorous incidents. In a dialogue about moderation, Socrates gets aroused when the robe of young Charmides falls open exposing his bare body. This amazing body gives promise of an equally amazing mind, worthy of a philosopher's lust. In the *Symposium* when Aristophanes employs Eryximachus' cure for his hiccups, he does this publicly while Eryximachus drones on with his speech. One must picture Aristophanes with the exaggerated flair of a comic, holding his breath through various shades of turning purple, gargling at the top of his volume and then building up slowly but surely to the grand finale of the sneeze. All this happens while the doctor describes how he has learned through his science to control human bodies. The *Euthydemus* is full of silliness with the two wrestling coaches turned rhetoric teachers eager to display and describe their skills as though they were still in the ring.

There is one other literary source for the dialogue form, Socrates himself. Although he never wrote anything about how he conducted his philosophical pursuits, we know from several historical sources that he engaged others in conversations. Some of these became famous enough, according to the opening conversation in Plato's *Symposium*, that people would request to hear particularly famous conversations. That Xenophon wrote an *Apology* and *Symposium* as well as Plato gives further evidence that Socrates' dialogue style at these events was well known. Xenophon recounts other Socratic conversations in his *Memorabilia*, and other writers such as Aischines were reputed also to have written such accounts. These written dialogues starring Socrates were not so much a literary genre as a means by his friends and followers to record the events of his life and maintain his memory.

The Platonic dialogues, then, are not the only variety of their kind in ancient Athens. There are other Socratic dialogues, and there are other dramatized historical debates and discussions. There are also more modern dialogues written by philosophers, such as those of Hume and Berkeley, but these seem rather two-dimensional, lacking the drama which, perhaps, grew out of the richer cultural soil of ancient Athens. We are now ready to examine some specific elements of these dialogues to see how they work and contribute to the whole.

II. Frames and Settings

In this section we will examine some of the dramatic devices in the dialogues and then in the following ones discuss how the conversations work, the role of the stories and myths and finally a brief look at Socratic irony. The best way to see how these dramatic elements work philosophically is to examine a dialogue in detail, a task for which the present book is too short. A good introductory level book is Koyre's *Discovering Plato*, which discusses the *Meno, Protagoras, Republic* and *Theaetetus*.[4] In this section we will identify some of the writing devices which Plato uses and see how they function.

An important point to remember is to keep track of one's emotional responses as well as the logical ones. The characters in the dialogues are full of emotions. Mostly they get angry with Socrates when he defeats them, but they also get embarrassed and even blush (Thrasymachus (*Rep.* 350d) and Euthydemus' brother (297a)). They are in love (Lysis), fearful of their reputations (Crito) or of death (Cephalus), and worried about their children (Lysimachus and Melisias in the *Laches*). As Socrates works with his partners' responses, so Plato works with ours. It is often only after the emotions have been released that the ideas they have been defending are exposed and able to be examined. Just as we saw rhetoric can be used as a symptom to help us recognize the defenses we use to shield our ideas, so can emotions help identify such defenses.

Although most dialogues stand alone, three groups of dialogues are dramatically connected. The *Republic* seems to be Socrates' contribution to an agreement among three other friends that each will tell a story. The *Timaeus* and the *Critias* are two more in this series, while we have no record of any dialogue from the fourth partner Hermocrates. The group active in the *Theaetetus* gathers the next day for the *Sophist* and *Statesman*. At the end of the *Theaetetus* Socrates says he must go to the court of the King-Archon to answer charges brought against him. This ties this dialogue to the series connected with his trial and execution, the *Euthyphro, Apology, Crito*, and *Phaedo*. The degree to which the meaning of one dialogue in a group is elaborated by the others has been debated for centuries.

Amid the great variety of settings and modes of presentation in the dialogues, there are dominant styles in many areas. Two-thirds take place in a well-defined setting. Three-fourths take place in a group of over two people. Two-thirds use direct narration by an anonymous and invisible narrator. But none of these majorities coincide. Plato frequently shifts his style of presentation. We must pay attention to each dialogue to determine why these elements are used in this situation. In the eight dialogues where Socrates is alone with his partner, what does this intimacy have to do with the content? In the *Phaedrus*, for instance, Socrates and Phaedrus are alone in an isolated romantic spot where a god was said to have ravished a young girl (229). Phaedrus, whose body attracts many love letters, is coyly provocative, but Socrates uses this steamy context to discuss the seductiveness not of bodies but of speeches, such as the one Phaedrus is memorizing. The occasion is perfect for using our physical sexual lives as an image to examine our mental sex lives. Mental rape is what concerns Socrates here, to impregnate another with an idea that will take hold and grow in him. As this belief matures, he considers this brainchild to be his own, and suffers the inability of all parents to properly assess their children.

This sexuality of ideas theme reappears in many of the dialogues. In the opening of the *Protagoras* Socrates' young friend is in danger of becoming like the sophist whose ideas (children) he hopes to carry away inside him, while in the *Theaetetus* Socrates describes himself as a midwife who helps others pregnant with an idea to bring it into the light of day to see if this new idea is whole and healthy or just hot air (149a-151d).[5] In the *Symposium* the self-proclaimed homosexual superiority of this all-male party is questioned by Diotima's speech as she as opposes the need for procreation to the sterility of homosexual activity. Here the description of our mental lives emphasizes the need for contact with different ideas with its possibility of cross-fertilization. It also reminds us that Socrates always attacks the center of his opponent's ego, which for this group is their homosexual maleness, and culminates here in his refusal to have sex with Alcibiades, destroying the latter's idea of the good, himself.

Most of the stories have a definite setting that reflects the ideas under discussion and reveals the consequences of holding these ideas. Religious beliefs have political consequences in the *Euthyphro, Apology* and *Phaedo*. What you love influences what you become, as the seven speakers illustrate in the *Symposium*. The *Republic* takes place in the Piraeus, Athens' seaport, which attracts new immigrants, religions, and ideas, a place of civic instability and rootlessness where Socrates can be waylaid but also revolutionary ideas can be developed outside the city's traditions. Phaedrus in his dialogue is similarly in an environment of change, pursuing a new exercise program and a new speech. Ideas present Euthydemus and his brother with a new arena for wrestling. Cephalus comes to Athens to hear the story of Parmenides who, ironically, believed motion was impossible.

For a number of the dialogues the setting is just after a sophistic demonstration. Socrates sees the exhibitions in *Euthydemus, Laches,* and *Hippias Minor* and arrives just after Gorgias, Protagoras, Cratylus, and Ion have given theirs. This competitive environment is also present in the several dialogues set in the gymnasia and wrestling schools. Socrates initially refuses to participate in such exhibitions but often ends up doing something similar as in the long interpretation of Simonides' poem in the *Protagoras*, trading etymologies with Cratylus in his dialogue, quoting long passages from Homer with Ion the rhapsode, and capping the rhetoric of Lysias' speech with his own in the *Phaedrus*. He is like a chameleon, blending enough with his partners to use their terms and arguments, the better ultimately to engage them in criticism.

In five dialogues Plato uses a more complicated framing technique to set the story within another story. In the framing story two people are discussing the main action after it has occurred, with one of them anxious to hear exactly what took place. Only in the *Phaedo*, however, is the subject of their interest Socrates. Cephalus in the *Parmenides* comes to Athens with friends from Clazomenae to hear Plato's brother recite the encounter between Parmenides and the youthful Socrates. In the *Symposium* a friend wants to hear a racy story to help occupy a tedious walk. The *Theaetetus* is presented as a reminiscence of its dying namesake. And the companion in the *Protagoras* wants the latest news of the sophist. Few of the dialogues are presented as philosophical encounters. They are usually people looking for a good story or discussion, and Socrates turns the talk to philosophy.

We as readers always come to any work with our own frame of reference, and Plato here uses his frames to call to our attention the consequences of these frames for what occurs within them. This is most elaborately developed in the opening of the *Symposium*. Apollodorus, a highly wrought groupie of Socrates, tells the story he heard from another groupie, Aristodemus, to a non-philosopher companion as they walk to town.[6] Apollodorus explains why his story should be believed. He creates his own little pre-story, reflecting Plato's use of this whole episode as his own pre-story to introduce this dialogue. Apollodorus explains how he has just told this story two days ago and relates how Glaucon came looking for him as someone who should know what happened, since he is a devoted follower of Socrates and checked out the facts with him. He does admit that the events took place when he was only a boy and his version of them he received from Aristodemus who was at the party. It also gives him the chance to mention that an inferior version told by Phoenix is also in circulation. Apollodorus then directly speaks to today's companion, praising the pleasures of philosophy over this man's business concerns. The friend returns this mild insult by recalling Apollodorus' nickname of fanatic. When Apollodorus finally begins his story, he promises to retell all he was told, but within a few pages he says "Aristodemus did not recollect precisely everything that each speaker said, and I do not recollect everything that Aristodemus told me, but I will tell you the most important points in each of the speeches that seemed to me worth remembering" (178a). (So much for recollection.)

Today's conversation is framed by the events of two days ago, just like the party itself is framed by Agathon's victory and first drunken party two days ago. The sequence is, Agathon's victory-Agathon's party-Aristodemus tells the story-Apollodorus tells the story two days ago- Apollodorus tells the story today. The recital by Apollodorus is further framed by the faulty memories of Apollodorus and Aristodemus and the non-critical listening of the companion. The elaborate setting of this scene helps us consider our own settings and memories. Reports of other people's events and ideas can never be directly communicated; there is always some principle of selection at work. Our ideas similarly have histories that influence what we think they mean. The frames remind us of our distance from the events being retold and that merely repeating the great philosopher's words will not overcome this, while engaging in the criticism of these ideas might revive them.

III. Conversation

Plato's conversations in the dialogues are between real people, and we need to investigate who these people are and how their talk proceeds. These people have real intentions, habits, desires, emotions, prejudices, reputations, expectations, attachments, etc. They have personalities and follow these in their speech and actions. They do not behave as they do merely for the convenience of Plato's plot or his philosophy. For instance, a character will often respond to Socrates with a series of short affirmative answers. This is not Plato using the character to gain our agreement as well, but rather showing us how the character thinks. Some editors, notably Cornford in his edition of the *Republic*,[7] believe that these extended stretches of minimal response by Socrates' partner can safely be removed from the text. These long stretches of "yes, certainly, that's so, plainly," etc. help establish the tempo of the experience, showing not only the character's way in the story but also the reader's way of following the text, the conversation we are having with Plato. We nod our heads until roused from our "copy" program by something catching our interest, either the sublime or the ridiculous. Then our response becomes an emphatic "No!" or "Yes!" and the engagement begins anew. This reflects our general reluctance to disturb an authority, as when Simmias and Cebes defer disturbing the condemned Socrates and thus also defer having to think for themselves.

The people involved in these conversations with Socrates are rarely philosophers, with the exceptions of Parmenides in his dialogue and his later follower, the Eleatic Stranger. There are some famous sophists, as Gorgias, Hippias and Protagoras, and some less famous ones, as Thrasymachus and Callicles, and some ridiculous ones such as Euthydemus and his brother. There are soldiers as Meno, Alcibiades, Polemarchus, Laches, Nicias, and Plato's brothers Glaucon and Adeimantus. There are young men full of promise, as Charmides, Theaetetus, Lysis, Menexenus, Philebus, and those not so promising, as Phaedrus. There is Euthyphro, a self-proclaimed religious seer, Ion, a rhapsode who performs the Homeric poems, and Lysias, a speechwriter for all occasions from law courts to love courting. There is Timaeus bringing his ideas about nature from Italy. There are old men offering the wisdom of their experience, as Crito and Critias and the Cretan, Spartan and Athenian in the *Laws*.

There are many types of people in the dialogues but few philosophers or displays of philosophical competition where the criticism of ideas is the agenda for evenly matched sides. Rather the dialogues most often start from a question about one of life's common problems: how to succeed, to raise children, to know a friendship will last, to face death, to recognize justice or love or a sophist or statesman, in general, how to live better rather than worse and to appear smart and not foolish. Socrates' response is to nudge his partner out of a piecemeal approach to the problem toward a more comprehensive examination of the basic ideas and terms involved and their connections with other ideas that we hold. This process is called "dialectic", which generally means to converse or argue and more specifically to examine the connections between ideas. "The inquiry into all the things we have gone through (justice, the polis and the soul) arrives at their community and relationship with one another, and draws conclusions as to how they are akin to one another, and then the concern with them contributes something to what we want" (*Republic* 531c-d). In the *Phaedrus* Socrates describes the two methods in this reasoning.

> The first method is to take a synoptic view of many scattered
> particulars and collect them under a single generic term, so as
> to form a definition in each case and make clear the exact
> nature of the subject one proposes to expound... That
> definition may have been good or bad, but at least it enabled
> the argument to proceed with clearness and consistency... (The
> other method is) the ability to divide a genus into species
> again, observing the natural articulation, not mangling any of
> the parts, like an unskillful butcher... I am a great lover of
> these methods of division and collection as instruments which
> enable me to speak and to think (and) have given those who
> possess this ability the title of dialecticians. (265d-266c)

The dialogues show these methods starting from the simple questions posed by the partners and then demonstrating the need for a more
comprehensive inquiry. The vehicle for the first of these methods is
usually some broad value term, such as one of the virtues, a human
relation, such as friendship, or an emotion, such as desire for pleasure
or fear of death. Socrates uses the specific problem to raise questions
about the related foundational ideas, but the partner only wants a quick
band-aid and to get on with life. He wants to know how to succeed, not
to examine what success really is.

In order to discuss the second method, we need a short interlude
concerning the order and relative dates of composition for each of the
dialogues. This is one of those popular debates that the Preface warned
would be put off until needed, and now is the time. This has been a
major issue for the last two centuries of Platonic commentary and af-
fects how Plato's use of dialectic is discussed. We have already seen
how circular the arguments can be which depend on the order of composition in order to support specific interpretations, such as the development of Plato's ideas. Although it is claimed that the sequence is
supposed to determine the content, it is often content which is invoked
to justify the order of sequence. Stylometrics is the least circular of the
current dating arguments. It analyzes the frequency of specific elements in a person's writing style. This has permitted scholars to group
Plato's writings according to the presence or absence of these elements,
especially those so small as to be usually used with little attention. In
theory this accounting would reflect the writer's habits which would
change slowly and remain fairly stable for extended periods, thus permitting the grouping of dialogues which show similar habits of style.

There is a long tradition of dividing the dialogues into three such
periods. The early period shows Socrates seeking definitions of a word

like "justice," and the conversation ending without being able to find one. It is considered to reflect the words and actions of the historical Socrates. This has lead to the current debate about when Plato begins to write in his own voice; in which dialogue does the character Socrates drop his historical beliefs and become Plato's mouthpiece. Gregory Vlastos organized and inspired much of the inquiry in this area, and his writings should be consulted for more details.[8] The middle period shows greater dramatic complexity, with a less abrasive Socrates who moves beyond definition to dialectic and the partners more willing and able participants who are more satisfied with the conclusions attained. The later period seems more stark, with the drama less obvious, Socrates sometimes sitting on the sidelines or not even present as in the *Laws*, the partners becoming almost too willing or "tractable," and the philosophical analysis or dialectic more intense and center stage.

These divisions of the dialogues into time periods could equally well be considered as divisions into types of conversation, which might help us avoid turning claims of chronology into ones of development. Stylometrics can divide the dialogues into groups with similar styles but cannot demonstrate that these styles could only have occurred in a serial fashion, each example of a style having to belong to the same defined period of production. There are bodies of evidence to support these claims of distinct time periods, but there is no consensus on their necessary meaning. Plato could have revisited an earlier style in order to connect current work to some past theme or situation.

If we could describe these three different writing styles in other terms than time sequence, then we might avoid the temptation to assume a chronological support for our interpretations. The Greek word *sunousia* or "being with," may be useful here. Similar to our "intercourse," it describes either a conversation or a sexual encounter. We have seen Plato describe philosophy using such sexual language. The *Symposium* opens using this word to describe Agathon's drinking party as an "orgy," but the only sexual activity turns out to occur between ideas and words. Socrates' adventures in the dialogues might then be divided into three types of intercourse, 1) on the make, as Socrates tries to connect with his reluctant conversation partners, 2) in relationship, as he works through difficult issues with attentive partners, and 3) other lovers, where he takes a seat and lets others speak, or in sum, 1) seeking a partner, 2) having a partner, 3) changing partners.

Other thematic connections could be found as well to describe these stylistic groups in less restrictive ways for the philosophic unity of the dialogues than the current chronological and developmental divisions. I suggest calling these types "one, two and three," which roughly coincide with the current "early, middle, late" with respect to type of conversation and style. The following lists are alphabetical and should permit readers to follow the discussions that use such groupings.[9] The lists may vary from one commentator to the next.

Type One	Type Two	Type three
Alcibiades Major	*Phaedo*	*Critias*
Apology	*Phaedrus*	*Parmenides*
Charmides	*Republic*	*Philebus*
Clitophon	*Symposium*	*Sophist*
Cratylus		*Statesman*
Crito		*Theaetetus*
Euthydemus		*Timaeus*
Euthyphro		
Gorgias		*Laws* - generally
Hippias Major & Minor		assumed to be
Ion		written last
Laches		
Lysis		
Menexenus		
Meno		
Protagoras		

Now we can finish our discussion of dialectic. In the *Phaedrus* quote above Socrates spoke of two methods of reasoning. The first tries to discover the "one in the many", as the Greeks called the problem of definition. In the first type of dialogues this is Socrates' main question. What is virtue (*Meno*), moderation (*Charmides*), friendship (*Lysis*), piety (*Euthyphro*)? The second method tries to determine the relations and distinctions between the items to be defined. This is discussed as a method in the second type of conversations, as we saw in the *Republic* and the *Phaedrus* above, and demonstrated in the third. In the *Republic* several types of cities are constructed and five types of government are examined, but there is no effort to explain "city" or "government" by diaeresis, the complete classification of their defining features and distinguishing these from other similar ideas. This is the focus in the third type of conversations, like the search for the namesake of the *Sophist,* where different defining features are tested (angler, merchant, warrior) to see which will be most productive in trying to classify him.

This concern with the difficulties of definition is continuous throughout the dialogues. We have seen the journey to Hades to try to find such definitions and the medical interventions to evaluate their

80

health and cure them if they are diseased. We have seen definition as the playground of the rhetoricians, switching meanings between relative and absolute, individual and group, according to culture or to nature. It is also the ground of friendship between philosophers as they exchange and criticize each other's ideas. The Cave image at the end of the last chapter shows how difficult definition can be. Philosophy does not (and can not) enter the *Republic* until criticism is present, until after the young men raise the problems which Socrates calls "the three waves" in Book V (457c, 457d, 472a). The effort to clarify the definitions becomes philosophical only after the philosophers have been educated and can follow the three images: the Sun helping us realize the life-defining and sustaining power of the idea of the good, the Line helping us see the mass of opinion and images with which we have to deal in order to distinguish these from knowledge, and the Cave showing that the connections to these opinions and images are not just intellectual but pervade our lives and require a conscious removal from these connections in order to examine our foundational ideas such as that of the good.

This concern with definition leads us to the last topic in this section, the Theory of Forms. The development and elaboration of this Theory has attracted more attention in the last fifty years than any other area of Platonic scholarship and must be approached with the due caution Shorey recommended in the introductory quotation for this chapter. We sometimes enforce closure where Plato was suggestive and construct systems where he was hypothetical. Forms are discussed in the dialogues as the true definitions of things, somewhat on the parallel of geometric shapes. An absolutely straight line or a circle with every circumference point exactly equidistant from its center could never be drawn and thus never be physically seen. But we can understand such a concept and even see it "with the mind's eye."

This term "form" shares this conflation of knowing and seeing. It can be confusing, as it is used to describe something conceptual (definition) as well as perceptual (the shape of a thing). In Greek this ambiguity is part of the word *eidos* itself, which has two branches of meanings, things seen and things known. This ambiguity played an active role in Greek intellectual life, as it has ever since. The tragedy "Oedipus Rex", for example, turns on the hero's inability to be able to know the truth about what he sees. The blind wise man Teiresias is able to "see" more clearly and recognize Oedipus' untenable situation as both husband and son to the same woman. And Sophocles maintains a steady cadence of variations of *eidos* to hold this relation of seeing and knowing before us during the play. [10]

The Greeks connected these phenomena because forms are a psychological reality. We picture things to ourselves, from daydreams about a vacation to definitions about the good. Most of these images are clear, as my idea of the next words I am going to type. Some are quite vague, especially those loaded with conflict, such as the ideal child or parent. Plato keeps calling our attention to this connection, as in the geometry problem in the *Meno*, where the answer is a line that can be seen yet not precisely described as its length is an irrational number. This parallels their search for virtue, where Socrates and Meno agree that they have seen virtuous people yet seem unable to describe exactly what this quality is. Socrates' repeated use of images in his arguments also builds on this psychological foundation. He is encouraging people to see his ideas and to search more diligently (the hunting metaphors) for their own.

The form thus presents an ideal answer in the ideal world of our minds. The circles and triangles in our minds are the real things as they can do all the things they are supposed to. Our ideals of courage and love and chariots also do all the right things--in our minds. This is why we believe in them. The problem is how the ideal constructions of our minds compare with our interactions with the rest of the world.[11] To say that Plato chose the ideal over the real is a common and misleading simplification. Plato examines the construction and criticism of ideals in order to improve upon the "reals" which we currently believe and find inadequate. We then do choose the new ideal over the old real if it meets the test, as Socrates says, and more adequately explains our experience. To focus on the forms that we "see" is to emphasize both the need to test them and the possibility of finding more; thus they keep recurring when philosophy is being discussed.

IV. Stories and Myths

There is a tension in the relation of *muthos* (story, myth) and *logos* (reason, argument) in the dialogues. It is often unclear how they are similar and how different. When describing the afterlife in Hades at the end of the *Gorgias*, Socrates begins by saying "Then listen, as they say, to a very fine *logos*, which you may consider a *muthos*, but I regard as a *logos*; for I want you to take everything I shall say as truth" (523a) When he then explains the fate of an unjust person, he tells a story that he considers to be a good argument and true. Phaedo in his dialogue describes the activity of Socrates' last day as "engaged in philosophical discussion as we were accustomed to do" (59a). Yet Socrates describes his plan for the day as, "it is perhaps most appropriate for one who is about to depart yonder to mythologize and examine tales about what we believe that journey to be like" (61d-e). He then gives several arguments for the immortality of the soul. In the *Republic* when they are cleaning up the city's educational content, they begin with the stories about the gods because these become the arguments upon which we base our values later in life. In the *Symposium* when Socrates gives his *logos* on love, he does so by telling a story about his instruction in love by the divinely inspired Diotima. He claims that one subject he understands is love-matters (177e), and yet when he explains the origin and content of this knowledge, he uses a story instead of a rational account, even emphasizing its fictional nature. He includes pieces of all the previous speeches in his story, which Aristophanes realizes and comments upon (212c). Finally in the *Phaedrus* as they settle into their secluded spot outside the city, Phaedrus asks whether Socrates believes the myth which is told about this place. He responds that he does not have time to demythologize all these stories; there are too many of them, and it would be a full-time occupation. He already has the occupation given him by the Delphic oracle's admonition to know himself. He says that he "accepts the customary beliefs" about the traditional myths so he can dedicate his time to investigating himself.[12] And to do so, he re-mythologizes himself, wondering if he is "a monster more complex and furious than Typhon or a gentler and simpler creature" (230a).

Philosophers tend to take their arguments neat, preferably eliminating all the ambiguities of language by reducing the terms to symbols and allowing logic to have its way. Socrates seems to act contrary to this. When he needs an argument, he presents a story dressed up in extra language, and yet when he says he is presenting a story as a *logos*, his language can become very spare and direct as in the *Phaedo's* arguments or even better in the *Meno's* geometry problem. What is the role of *muthos* in the dialogues? Arguments are ways of making sure that we do know what we think we know, of fastening down our opinions that otherwise wander like Daedelus' statues in the *Meno*. Stories do not provide such logical proofs with premises and conclusions.

One thing they seem to provide here is more like hypotheses, positions from which to begin inquiry yet also positions to hold while waiting for something better to come along. There is no simple proof that the unjust person will be unhappy or happy in life. The story of the Ring of Gyges presents the argument for happiness; the description of the tyrant and the story of Er's visit to Hades present the argument for unhappiness. But the Er story presents another aspect of hypothesis that we saw earlier in all the reincarnation stories, that regardless of our previous life, we can take a position toward our life now and try it.

> I do not insist that my argument is right in all other aspects, but I would contend at all costs both in word and deed as far as I could that we will be better men, braver and less idle, if we believe that one must search for the things one does not know, rather than if we believe that it is not possible to find out what we do not know and that we must not look for it.
> (*Meno* 86b)

This is such a hypothesis, a position for which arguments can be developed, but none of them so far seem to be persuasive, as the continuing discussions through the dialogues whether philosophy is a fit activity for an adult make clear.[13]

Myths in the dialogues, then, present something that we should believe, not in the sense of unquestionable doctrines inculcated from youth, but as visions of how to live, which, as images, can be discussed and evaluated. One of my favorite (and therefore one of the best) stories in the dialogues is Aristophanes' speech in the *Symposium*. I will end this section by showing how his images can help us to focus the discussion and advance our ideas.

Aristophanes is the middle speaker at Agathon's party. The first three speakers have presented ideas of love taken from the traditional values of the poets, the cultural relativism and utilitarian values of the sophists or social scientists and the objective natural science of the medical man. Each self-destructs as Phaedrus wants to change what one of the poets said (scripture cannot be emended), Pausanias promises his beloved excellence but reserves the lover's right to lie, Eryximachus shows the supreme power of love in all things but then claims he has control over love of food and other medical matters. Each begins discussing love as a great force outside us (a goddess) but ends by subordinating this force to gratify his ego.

Aristophanes says he is going to take a new approach and discusses a love beyond our control, building on the ancient idea that somewhere there exists a mate just for me, my perfectly matched other half. He understands the human longing for completeness which the first three egos did not. He also understands our apparent inability to achieve this. His story describes how we were originally double people, with two bodies attached at the stomach, two faces on one head, two sets of genitals on the outside for external fertilization "like grasshoppers", four arms and legs, etc. These people tried to gain the gods' power and were punished by being split in half, thus creating us. If we don't be-have, we will be split again, rendering our mouths and sex organs, among other things, inoperable. As a result of the split, our stomachs were sewn up leaving the navel, our heads turned around (remember the Cave), and our genitals put in front so we could at least experience the wholeness of the old days when we copulate.

But how do we find our other half? We have to get together with someone and experience the fit. If it is the best fit there could possibly be, then this is our one and only. But after seeing more of the world, we might think our previous judgment too hasty, for some pretty good-looking fits have come to our attention. We try a few and find one that is everything we ever imagined. And then our imagination moves on, and we begin again to wonder whether we are properly connected. Aristophanes' idea is to spend our lives going belly-to-belly with every other person in the world in order to finally judge which is the best fit. And I hope you can remember #302,783 when you are engaged with #80,436,924 in order to be able to properly compare. What are the sig-nificant criteria that one should keep track of--what is the diaerisis of "fit?" Aristophanes' story breaks down on the physical level (so many bodies, so little time) and drives us on to the philosophical level. Aris-tophanes is the first at the party to define love, saying it is "simply the name for the desire and pursuit of the whole" (193a). This is how Soc-rates is spending his life, looking for someone to help him find com-pletion, to share his views, his ideas, his criticisms--even his Forms.

V. Socratic Irony

I will end this overview of Plato's writings with a few comments upon one last source of confusion in the dialogues, Socrates' irony. The problems here are similar to those experienced by us when a teacher attempts to use the Socratic method. If the teacher does know the an-swer, why doesn't she just say it instead of playing "Twenty Ques-tions," and if she does not, how is the class ever going to find something that she has not been able to find? Warning bells from Meno's "learning paradox" (one either already knows it or never will) should be going off. Socratic method often seems like a waste of time with the teacher hiding behind a veil of false ignorance in order to lead the class to make some predetermined discovery.[14] This method seems to work best only when there is a possibility that something new may actually be discovered. The teacher certainly knows much and could give an adequate answer, but it is exciting to see if there may not be an even better response waiting to be spoken. And in turn, of course, to test whether it really is better.

It is the same with Socratic irony. Irony suggests some sort of doubling in the meaning of what one says, either additionally meaning less, as when telling someone who has been insulting to "have a *nice* day", or meaning more, as when speaking of a funhouse ride in which one gets pushed out of the exit, "you will get a real *kick* out of it." When Socrates responds to the uncooperative, he may sound sarcastic and nasty as the former, while with those too ready to believe him, he seems to make them work through the multiple meanings in order to appreciate better the complexity of the problem. This is how Friedlander describes Socrates' use of irony.

> The concept (of irony) may waver between dissimulation, hated or despised, playful hide and seek (a common idiom of the intellectually brilliant and critically suspicious society of democratic Athens), and dangerous concealment, feared or admired. Indeed, friends as well as enemies could talk about Socrates' irony with very different meanings.[15]

In this third category of concealment, the listener is made to feel uneasy, that there is something more happening but not quite like anything that is already known. This is when the irony, like the Socratic method above, can help lead the listener into a whole new category of possibilities where the search continues on a more complex level. The ironist does not know the answer; she knows what does not work and where one might be able to inquire further. Friedlander explains this further.

> Socratic irony, at its center, expresses the tension between ignorance--that is, the impossibility to put into words "what justice is"--and the direct experience of the unknown, the existence of the just man, whom justice raises to the level of the divine." [16]

We can see that there is something we call just or a sophist or the diagonal of the square in the *Meno*, yet these cannot be so simply described, as we have seen. The ironist may be more advanced in the inquiry, knowing more of what does not work, yet also realizing that her listeners need to go through the experience of these not working in order to understand the inquiry. For common sense that expects inquiry always to result in a simple answer, philosophy seems like an unnecessary multiplication of puzzles and pursued only for the pleasure of those who like such puzzles.

This is what Clitophon accuses Socrates of doing in the dialogue with his name. This shortest of the dialogues offers a critique of Socratic irony and method, just as the *Parmenides* offers one of the Forms. Socrates keeps getting people ready to do philosophy, to take care of their souls by defining key terms such as justice and then becoming just. But they never get to the definition, much less the action. Socrates is all talk, and it seems so only for the sake of talk. This is Clitophon's wonderfully accurate imitation of Socrates' stump speech, pestering his audience to accept a philosophical life.

> You say that men are unjust because they want to be, not
> because they are ignorant or uneducated. But then you have the
> effrontery to say, on the other hand, that injustice is shameful
> and hateful to the gods. Well, then, how could anyone
> willingly choose such an evil?! "Perhaps he is defeated by
> pleasure," you say. But isn't this defeat involuntary if
> conquering is voluntary? Thus every way you look at it, the
> argument shows that injustice is involuntary, and that every
> man privately and every city publicly must devote to this
> matter greater care than is presently the norm. (407d-e)

Clitophon claims with apparent irony to have accepted Socrates' call and then goes about questioning his followers hoping to find out more about this justice so he could start doing it.

> O you most distinguished gentlemen, what are we actually to
> make of Socrates' exhorting of us to pursue virtue? Are we to
> believe that this is all there is, and that it is impossible to
> pursue the matter further and grasp it fully? Will this be our
> life-long work, simply to convert to the pursuit of virtue those
> who have not yet been converted so that they in turn may
> convert others? Even if we agree that this is what a man should
> do, should we not also ask Socrates, and each other, what the
> next step is? How should we begin to learn what justice is?
> What do we say? (408d-e)

Since neither Socrates nor his followers could give him the kind of answers he wanted, Clitophon comes to this conclusion, which is shared by many other readers.

When I had endured this disappointment, not once or twice but
a long time, I finally got tired of begging for an answer. I came
to the conclusion that while you're better than anyone at
turning a man towards the pursuit of virtue, one of two things
must be the case: either this is all you can do, nothing more--as
might happen with any other skill, for example, when someone
who's not a pilot rehearses a speech in praise of the pilot's skill
as being something of great worth to men; the same could also
be done for any other skill. And someone might accuse you of
being in the same position with justice, that your ability to
praise it so well does not make you any more knowledgeable
about it. Now that's not my own view, but there are only two
possibilities: either you don't know it, or you don't wish to
share it with me... You're worth the world to someone who
hasn't yet been converted to the pursuit of virtue, to someone
who's already been converted you rather get in the way of his
attaining happiness by reaching the goal of virtue. (410b-e)

One of the simplistic divisions of the dialogues is between the
Socratic ones that end with such an *aporia* (impasse) as Clitophon
complains of and the Platonic ones where Plato delivers the answers
Clitophon wants. Some people even think this dialogue, if genuine,
may be the transition between the two phases of Plato's writings, lead-
ing up to the *Republic* where Clitophon also appears and justice is defined. I think this division reflects our sharing Clitophon's desire for
answers more than any change in the dialogues. We do find justice in
the *Republic* and love in the *Symposium* and the sophist in his dialogue,
but we find these within complex webs of particular conditions, reconstructions of ideas and attempted proofs that do not ultimately work.
There may be a difference between simpler and more complex invita-
tions to inquiry, but all the dialogues seek to enrich the inquiry to make
it as complex as the life situations it seeks to explain rather than simpli-
fying for the sake of an answer or an action.

And yet Clitophon should get some answer. What is the good of all
this preparatory behavior? We discussed earlier that philosophy is a
communal activity, and inquiry, with its intrinsic need for shared criticism, guarantees the community much better than answers which can
be packaged and carried away to be used however the individual so
desires, like the rhetorical tricks one has paid for. Answers freed from
inquiry put an end to philosophy, and with it an end both to the need
for a democratic social order, where everyone out of self-interest shares

information and arguments, and to basic truth-telling, which is our only hope of receiving truth in return.

Clitophon in the *Republic* does not believe that there is any truth in a situation or a speech other than that which someone, preferably himself, can impose upon it. His beliefs give him all the answers he will ever need. He is the measure of all things, so that what he *believes* to be to his advantage really is to his advantage. (340b) He cannot be influenced by what Socrates or anyone else says, and so his response to all further discussion is silence. This is the world of the tyrant, which at first seems to be filled with great noises, the demands of the constant stream of desires and the seductions of the constant stream of efforts to fulfill them. But at the center of this activity is Clitophon's same silence. There is no *logos* in the world of pure desire; it here has nothing to say. If our life is to be more than a leaky jar and our inquiry is to advance beyond silence, then we need to carefully consider Socrates' invitation to join in the development of the mutually critical philosophic community. The dialogues discuss the many difficulties of such citizenship but also one of its chief rewards, that when called upon to give an account of one's life, to give one's *apology*, one will have something to say.

Notes

1. Paul Shorey, *Platonism Ancient and Modern* (Berkeley: University of California Press, 1938), 23.
2. Commentators debate whether about six or so of the dialogues are genuine or not, and this makes the list of dialogues vary from one to the next. Friedlander counts 31. Cooper counts 26 plus three more as probably genuine. Taylor counts 27.
3. One could include all of the speeches in the *Symposium* as an autobiographical series, recounting the intellectual journey of Plato's life up to the critical moment when he like Alcibiades had to decide whether criticism or desire was more important in his life.
4. Alexandre Koyre, *Discovering Plato*, (New York, Columbia University Press, 1945). Paul Friedlander's *Plato*, 3 vols. (Princeton: Princeton University Press, 1969) discusses all of the dialogues. Charles Griswold *Self-Knowledge in Plato's Phaedrus* (New Haven: Yale, 1986) is a good example of examining a single dialogue.
5. Benjamin Jowett's translation uses the wonderful Victorian expression "wind egg" to describe this internal hot air, which we mistake for being pregnant. It is worthwhile to read a variety of translations in or-

der to avoid being held hostage by the translator's ideas of what Plato must have meant or the proper language for philosophy.

Plato, *Theaetetus*, trans. Jowett, (Indianapolis: Bobbs-Merrill, 1949)

6. Aristodemus tries to be Socrates by looking and acting like him. He goes barefoot and arrives at Agathon's as the physical surrogate for Socrates. Apollodorus tries to be Socrates by saying his words. His business is to "know what Socrates says and does every day" (172c).

7. F. M. Cornford, *The Republic of Plato* (New York: Penguin, 1945) Preface.

8. Vlastos lived a long and productive life, publishing for over 40 years. A good example of his work in this area is "Socrates." *Proceedings of the British Academy* 74:87-109.

9. Once again Brandwood offers a good discussion of stylometrics.

10. Roochnik in his *Tragedy of Reason* uses the Oedipus story to illustrate the need of reason to know, in which the forms play a role, and the ultimate failure of reason to satisfy this need, especially on quality of life and moral issues.

11.   "You mean he will (be willing to mind the political things) in the city whose foundation we have now gone through, the one that has its place in speeches (logoi), since I don't suppose it exists anywhere on earth."
        "But in heaven (the sky)," I said, "perhaps, a pattern is laid up for the man who wants to see and found a city within himself on the basis of what he sees. It doesn't make a difference whether is or will be somewhere. For he would mind the things of this city alone, and of no other." *Republic* 592a-b.

This passage has been taken by many readers, including St. Augustine, as proposing an ideal realm not just preferable to this world but offering life as perfected. Our Christian-shaped sensibilities of living in this world based upon expectations of the next one make it too easy for us to drop the thread of reason and criticism which Socrates, like Theseus in the ancient myth, uses to find his way about the labyrinth of life. In the dialogues we do not construct these ideals because life has failed us, but rather because we want to improve on our lives in life. Ideals here are not a substitute for life; they are hypotheses to be tested.

12. Compare this with Descartes' acceptance of the culture he was raised in while waiting to discover a better one in Part Three of his *Discourse on Method.*

13. Callicles wants to beat some sense (note again the lack of any argument except force) into anyone who still does philosophy as an adult (*Gorgias* 485c-d), and Thrasymachus claims Socrates and his philoso-

phy is as immature as an infant still needing a wet nurse and regular feedings (*Rep.* 343a and 345b).

14. Since most teachers know the answers to the questions they ask, this may account for why they wait only a few seconds before answering most of them by themselves.

15, P. Friedlander, *Plato*, vol.1, (New York: Harper & Row, 1964) 138.

16. Ibid., 155.

Selected Bibliography

There are thousands of books and articles about the writings of Plato and how they should be read. A good place to continue this inquiry is the following three collections with large selections of helpful essays and extensive bibliographies.

C. Griswald, ed. *Platonic Writings, Platonic Readings.* New York: Routledge, 1988.

R. Kraut, ed. *The Cambridge Companion to Plato.* New York: Cambridge University Press, 1992.

H. Benson, ed. *Essays on the Philosophy of Socrates.* New York, Oxford University Press, 1992.

Overviews of Plato's life and work:

G. C. Field. *Plato and his Contemporaries: A Study in Fourth Century Life and Thought.* 3rd ed. London: Metheun, 1967.

P. Friedlander. *Plato.* Tr. H. Meyerhoff. 3 vols. Reprint. Princeton: Princeton University Press, 1973. .

G.M.A. Grube. *Plato's Thought.* Indianapolis: Hackett, 1980.

J.H. Randall. *Plato: Dramatist of the Life of Reason.* New York: Columbia University Press, 1970.

P. Shorey. *What Plato Said.* Chicago: University of Chicago Press, 1933

The Unity of Plato's Thought. Chicago: University of Chicago Press, 1960.

A.E. Taylor. *Plato: The Man and his Work.* London: Methuen, 1948.

G. Vlastos. *Platonic Studies.* 2nd ed. Princeton: Princeton University Press, 1981.

Books which I found particularly stimulating and helpful:

H. Cherniss. *The Riddle of the Early Academy.* Berkeley, University of California Press, 1945.

E. R. Dodds. *The Greeks and the Irrational.* Berkeley: University of California Press. 1951.

C. Griswold. Self-Knowledge in Plato's Phaedrus. New Haven: Yale University Press, 1986.

D. Hyland. *Finitude and Transcendence in the Platonic Dialogues.* New York: State University of New York Press, 1995.

A. Koyre. *Discovering Plato.* New York: Columbia University Press, 1945.

Martha Nussbaum. *The Fragility of Goodness: Luck and Ethics in Greek Tragedy and Philosophy.* Cambridge: Cambridge University Press, 1986.

D. Roochnik. *The Tragedy of Reason.* New York: Routledge, 1990.

S. Rosen. *Plato's Symposium.* 2nd ed. New Haven: Yale University Press, 19867

K. Seeskin. *Dialogue and Discovery: A Study in Socratic Method.* Albany: State University of New York Press, 1987.

H. L. Sinaiko. *Love, Knowledge, and Discourse in Plato: Dialogue and Dialectic in Phaedrus, Republic, and Parmenides.* Chicago: University of Chicago Press, 1965.

F. Solmsen. *Intellectual Experiments of the Greek Enlightenment.* Princeton: Princeton University Press, 1975.

R. K. Sprague. *Plato's Use of Fallacy: A Study of the Euthydemus and Some Other Dialogues.* New York: Barnes and Noble, 1962.

M. Stokes. *Plato's Socratic Conversations: Drama and Dialectic in Three Dialogues.* Baltimore: Johns Hopkins University Press, 1986.

E. Tigerstedt. *Interpreting Plato.* Uppsala: Almquist & Wiksell International, 1977.